After The Podium

How to win after sports

Valeria Tsoy

Valeria Tsoy

Copyright © 2023 by Valeria Tsoy

All rights reserved.

No portion of this book may be reproduced in any form without written permission from the publisher or author, except as permitted by U.S. copyright law or Canadian copyright law.

This publication is designed to provide accurate and authoritative information in regard to the subject matter covered. It is sold with the understanding that neither the author nor the publisher is engaged in rendering legal, investment, accounting or other professional services. While the publisher and author have used their best efforts in preparing this book, they make no representations or warranties with respect to the accuracy or completeness of the contents of this book and specifically disclaim any implied warranties of merchantability or fitness for a particular purpose. No warranty may be created or extended by sales representatives or written sales materials. The advice and strategies contained herein may not be suitable for your situation. You should consult with a professional when appropriate. Neither the publisher nor the author shall be liable for any loss of profit or any other commercial damages, including but not limited to special, incidental, consequential, personal, or other damages.

Book Cover by Erika Orlova

Contents

INTRODUCTION.	5
PART I	1
CHAPTER 1	1
BY DEFAULT	1
CHAPTER 2	10
TRANSITION	10
CHAPTER 3	28
REALITY CHECK	29
CHAPTER 4	35
AFFECTIVE BLOCKS	36
CHAPTER 5	45
CONNECTED.	45
CHAPTER 6	79
II TYPES	79
CHAPTER 7	95
FROZEN	95
CHAPTER 8	117
WHO IS RESPONSIBLE?	117
CHAPTER 9	124
THE CURSE OF SUCCESS	124
CHAPTER 10	132

ATHLETES AND AGRESSION	132
CHAPTER 11	**136**
CAN I?	136
CHAPTER 12	**150**
WOMEN IN SPORTS	150
CHAPTER 13	**166**
ATHLETIC MOTHERS	166
CHAPTER 14	**172**
INTERPERSONAL NETWORK	172
PART II	**180**
CHAPTER 15	**180**
THE PACK	180
CHAPTER 16	**188**
NATURE VS NURTURE	188

After the Podium

Introduction.

Behold! This material results from years of intense research, self-reflection, and pondering. I don't want to bore you with any fluff, so I'll cut straight to the juicy bits.

But first, let's tackle the age-old question: who is an athlete? Please take a moment to visualize your ideal athlete and all the glorious traits they possess. Are they a chiseled Adonis with rippling muscles? Or a fierce competitor with the heart of a lion? Whatever it is, hold onto that image like as we set our point A.

Now, let's hop in our time machine and travel back to ancient Rome and Greece - where it all began. The original Olympic Games may have been shrouded in mystery, but we can safely assume that most contestants were battle-hardened soldiers and slaves. Yikes. These games were a distraction from the harsh realities of life and a way for the government to gain some appreciation from the masses and contain its dissatisfaction with the reining power.

And let's not forget the brutal fights between men and animals. It was like a real-life version of "Jumanji," except it was life or death instead of a board game. Survival was reserved for the elite warriors,

Valeria Tsoy

but even they couldn't escape the physical toll of constant warfare. Retirement was a pipe dream for these guys - they were lucky to survive past 30.

So, there you have it, guys - a brief history of athletic brutality. Stay tuned for more riveting insights and witty anecdotes in the pages to come.

Don't think it's all doom and gloom. Just relax and enjoy the ride.

Ah, the Olympics - the world's favorite way to watch people run, jump, and throw things without being labelled as "creepy." But did you know that athletes used to have "owners" like a fancy racehorse? Yup, wealthy businessmen would train their athletes from an early age to compete and make money for the owner.

After a 1500-year hiatus, the Olympics were reintroduced to the public. And boy, did they come back with a vengeance.

There were no games during the First or Second World War. Most of our interest gains a period after World War II.

The Cold War between the USA and USSR was in full swing, and what better way to show off your weapons than through the human body and its potential? It was like a science experiment gone wild - with athletes being raised in inhumane training environments like Sparta and patriotism being instilled from an early age. And let's not

After the Podium

forget the collateral damage - the athletes who sacrificed their bodies and lives for the "greater good." Talk about taking one for the team.

If originally Olympic Games were introduced as a festival, after 1947, it became heavily politicized. Some might argue that it still is, even though the Cold War supposedly ended after USSR's collapse. The Olympic Games were no longer a festival. They became a Warfield.

Only a few people know that many of the athletes on the USSR team were orphans and children from low-income families who couldn't take care of them and would give them up to sports Internauts. Facilities where biological weapons, a.k.a. athletes, the "made of steel," were raised.

The unbeatable Soviet athletes. For many children, becoming an athlete was the only way. Whether it was to escape a family of alcoholics and abuse or to get out of poverty and have food and shelter, many of these children had nothing to lose, so they would sacrifice themselves and their lives to "serve the country." Of course, Soviet athletes weren't just orphans; there were children from the middle class too.

Sports were free or at least funded by the government, so parents didn't need to choose whether it would be the food on the table or supporting their child's passion and talent. USSR was raising a healthy nation where traditional and non-traditional medicine walked hand-in-hand. It was also an excellent way to keep in touch with the demographics and recruit talents, who were then advanced to national and Olympic teams.

Today non-traditional medicine is fancily called biohacking. Where truthfully, it's real-life experiments of trial and error with the human body outside of a lab. Space science was being developed around the same time, so astronauts were trying things out. The human body had to withstand and function throughout the challenges of space and spaceships. Techniques were passed down and continued to develop in high-performance sports and the military. The human body became one of the most valuable tools in the progress of technology and science. Pushing the limit of the human body has always been praised by every society. Don't we all want to be some super-human, or what?

You bet the body is in a fight-or-flight state when it is forced to disregard the self-preservation instinct, which is exactly the quality a soldier needs on a battlefield.

How would you know if your body actually crossed the self-preservation limit? You would compare it to other bodies' abilities. If not a competition, which event would reach and measure results at its best? Internal competition is excellent.

We get to select the best ones out of our flock. But they all went through the same techniques and hacks. How do we know if what we're doing is the best possible? We put together an international competition.

Let's not forget about the other player in the cold war—the mighty USA.

The USA were also developing their human species. They wanted to prove their power and resources to the world and the USSR. Some sources claim that the US used psychological warfare on civilians after WWI to get the highest productivity and performance from the working class.

Edward Bernays, tasked with developing support tactics for World War I in the United States and other countries, realized that these tactics could be used during peacetime inside the nation. He later wrote a book in 1928 called "Propaganda," which became the handbook of men in power.

Sports and business became the invisible battlefield. In his book, Bernays wrote, "In almost every act of our daily lives, whether in this fear of politics or business, in our social contact or our ethical thinking, are dominated by the relatively small number of persons, that understand the mental processes and social patterns of the masses."

And while the Cold War was ongoing, there was no better way to test new tactics and compete civilly against the most significant

Valeria Tsoy

enemy than the Olympic games. It is a high-performance sport that also gave rise to doping. Therefore, it had to be prohibited or at least limited by the Olympic governing body. It was noticed that sports were becoming a bio-chemical lab, results-driven, with the mentality of "whatever it takes to win."

In the 20th century, we weren't savages anymore, but we still wanted the blood, the tears, and the show. So, the most fantastic competition of all time, The Olympic Games, started gaining popularity. In 1981 the Olympics were held in Moscow. The USA organized a boycott which was joined by 60 more countries. The US hired Boxing Star Muhammad Ali to campaign across Africa to recruit allies. He was met with lots of criticism and pushback. Being called a White House puppet made Muhammad Ali discontinue his pursuit.

For years, we have seen Sports being used as a political tool and a sign of power. Athletic accomplishments and medals are recognized and praised. Very similar to the war medals and military performance.

Let's face it - being an athlete is tough. You're like a superhero but without the cool gadgets and the cape. And you're constantly being pushed to your limits, just like your mom pushes you to eat your veggies. But at least you get to show off your skills to the world. And who knows, maybe you'll become a household name like Michael

After the Podium

Phelps or Simone Biles. Or maybe you'll end up like the majority of retired athletes searching for a new purpose in life.

When soldiers retire from service and can count on a pension, athletes are released from the sports world as non-useful material with nothing to fall back on.

So, what's the lesson here? Whether you're an athlete or not, it's essential to understand who you are and why you do the things you do. And if you ever find yourself being trained like a racehorse, maybe it's time to reconsider your career choices. Or, you know, just invest in some cool gadgets and a cape.

When studying athletes after retirement, I tried to collect a bigger wholesome picture by observing different areas of life.

99% of athletes showed dependency on an outside authority in one way or another. Reaching a goal was not a problem, yet distinguishing a meaningful pursuit was a struggle for almost everyone.

Clear vision and a plan design or alterations to the existing plan posed a hurdle and confusion.

Athletes who heavily depend on the system for values and morality are less likely to start their own businesses. They are more likely to become a 9-5 corp job employee. Younger athletes tend to be more willing to experiment with their location after sports. They often

Valeria Tsoy

employ the "throwing spaghetti at the wall" approach, hoping that something will stick. Very few people succeed with that, but almost everyone has or wants to try it.

No matter the athlete's achievement level, location, ethnicity, or employment status, the first step is always the same: pause and understand the processes during the sports career and after. Whom the athlete has become, why they do and feel the way they do and how it can be used in the best possible way to integrate into a new environment. In other words, even though it has ended, a sports career needs to reach its culmination through objective digesting and transition, which can only be done after the career ends.

Part I

Chapter 1

By Default

We are what we eat. You've heard that before, haven't you?

But we are also what we consume, namely, information.

Our mind is designed so that when offered two options, a full page of text and a page of images, we will choose the more straightforward option, in this case, images vs dense text.

Notice how kids' books primarily have pictures, whereas grown-ups can read 220 pages of plain text?

That's brain capacity and development for ya.

It's called the economics of the brain. Consumption of information requires brain energy. The brain automatically chooses more accessible options to preserve power.

Valeria Tsoy

Yup, our brains are lazy. And lazy brains are ironically efficient at preserving energy.

We see a rise in simplified content on social media to the point where it becomes primitive. We are regressing from critical and systemic thinking toward visual images.

Marcus E. Raichle, an American neurologist, identified three primary modes of thinking.

1. CEN, or Central Executive Network

2. SN, or Salience Network

3. DMN, or Default Mode Network.

The first mode is used when the brain is active and consumes information. The second mode is used for coordination in a situation and determining the significance of objects. The third mode, the Default Mode, is the most significant. It is when you get lost in thoughts, but if asked what you think about, you will likely respond, "Nothing."

This is when you develop brilliant problem solutions and the most creative ideas. It's the "a-ha"! Moment time.

After the Podium

In the first 25 years of our lives, our neuro cells develop connections in the brain, form neuro paths and build up our three modes of brain function. We are programming our brains. And we only have 25 years to build it up to its best potential.

Ashley C. Chen of Stanford University from the Department of Psychiatry and Behavioral Sciences pointed out that the modes we discussed earlier act as antagonists. That means that if SN or CEN modes are active (actively consuming), it suppresses the activity of the default system. This means that no energy goes toward the default system. When we actively consume information, the brain goes into hibernation.

Simply put, people, who spend their days on social media, think stereotyped and don't develop critical and creative thinking.

Gloria Mark, a professor in the Department of Informatics at the University of California, explained that for the default system to start working, it requires at least 23 minutes of no interruption to dive into a task.

Today, an average working adult is interrupted every 8 to 10 minutes, whether it is incoming text messages, emails, memos etc.

Evolutionary, the default system was created to develop social networks, so we can function as packs with the ability to communicate and adapt, skills necessary for survival.

There's a clear correlation between the amount spent using screens and social skills. The longer we are on screens, the fewer social skills we possess.

Some call our time the "Epidemic of Digital Autism."

It is characterized by

- Urge to check social media constantly

- Not understanding the feelings of others and not caring

- Lack of events and emotions in real life

- Not being interested in certain people, so they get replaced or "muted" instantly:

- Easier not to interact with people than adapt to their personalities

- Easier to interact via messages than in person

- Can't withstand extended psychological contact with each other

Researchers have proven that, just like alcohol, social media is a depressant. It raises social alertness, internal tensions, and conformism.

After the Podium

If that wasn't enough, in the era of the hyper-information environment, people lose their ability to envision the future. Our motivation and goals are directly impacted by our ability to form an image of the future.

Without the default system, we lose our chance of distal vision, and subsequently, we can't be motivated and can't set goals.

In the research of Ward and Bass in 2017, 3 groups of students were tested performing creative and thinking tasks.

1. Group was tested by having their phones in a different room

2. Group was tested having their phones nearby, like in the pocket or a bag

3. Group was tested with their phones facing down before them.

Hundreds of students engaged in testing. The research showed that the phone's physical location could impact our operative memory and our mind's flexibility.

A group with phones in a different room performed best. And the group with the phones on the table performed the worst. Do you want to check what's new in the world again?

Valeria Tsoy

We currently face division in our society, which is not only the rich and the poor but also the smart and the dumb.

These drives change in our interpersonal interactions with people around us.

Digital autism also impacts our physical skills of learning. Even if the information enters our brains, we don't have enough capacity to "digest" and decipher it.

Overeating is not only when it comes to food. Informational obesity is real.

With that, we face changes in communication and lower levels of emotional intelligence.

Our setting of instant gratification and inability to form images of the future leads to intolerance of people towards their mistakes and failures and hopes for quick and easy results.

Daniel Dennett, an American philosopher, writer, and cognitive scientist, said it very well.

"What is the problem with conveying tedious mental work to high-tech gizmos?

No problem if we somehow manage to prevent the atrophy of our cognitive skills".

After the Podium

Every invention out there is made to make our lives easier, but do we really need more of the "easy"?

Athletes today tend to have their phones in their pockets almost 24/7. Whether training or competing, they create content for themselves or the sponsors, broadcast on social media, switch music, or take pictures and videos.

The social media pandemic is, of course, impacting everyone with a smartphone. Yet, athletes, from an early age, get tiny opportunities to train the muscle of "tedious mental work," as physical work at that point is set as a prerogative.

In countries like Sweden, for example, students in grade 8 can choose their career path from grade 9 onward. Students who want to dedicate their lives to professional sports attend "sports high schools," depending on their sport. Technically, the prerequisite to the "school program" is Swedish and English languages. This eliminates up to 90% of the "mental" muscle training, which is fundamental. We only have up until 25 years old to train that muscle well enough, so we can use it for the rest of our lives in problem-solving, product and service development etc.

It's the time when the brain is going through its significant development; the athletes dive into the sports environment, being taught little about communication, social interaction, and general culture outside sports. The sports environment is concerned with the physical muscles first and foremost. It may not be their responsibility and their job to train anything else. Still, as a society, we need to take the bull by the horns to develop such mental skills in all community members. It is in our best interest, as the rest of the book will mention the "why" multiple times.

It's time we train brain muscles on par with our biceps.

We will always have the outliers who can become doctors and lawyers who were able to preserve their brain development after professional sports. Yet, here I am concerned with most athletes, who learn the skills and program their brains for the ways of the sports world. It is different from any other industry, except maybe the military. The skills necessary to be leaders, whether strategical or tactical, are not taught to athletes but are somehow expected by the public, employers, and even athletes themselves.

Social media hygiene is the first remedy to repair the default system and the ability to learn and perform "boring" tasks like reading or studying. It needs to be implemented in every household on par with dental hygiene. It took me about five months to regain my creative thinking after limiting social media to about 10 minutes daily. It was a path of definitive willpower training to recalibrate different brain areas.

We also need to be aware of our drive to simplify things, considering athletes' brains, especially young ones. Meditations are an excellent tool for training the default system. Yet, in my mind, the notion of "meditation" has been distorted by the Western world. Where a lot of the time, meditation is used as a relaxation tool versus a brain training tool. Different approaches yield different outcomes.

Athletes' brains are usually trained to achieve results. They are rarely trained to learn, reflect, and contemplate. Yet quick learning skill is paramount for the athlete after sports retirement, as that would directly impact their adaptability to a new environment and their self-reliance for financial stability. It would impact how they earn money, but also how they spend money.

Athletes are trained to power through discomfort and self-preservation instincts. I'd like to dive deep into how they can do that and how healthy it is.

Chapter 2

Transition

Transition is life in between. It's a space between two points: Before and after, birth and death, not yet and not anymore.

Athletes often need more skill to determine what fits them and where they fit. Usually, they know only one structure. The sports structure. They must adjust once, know the ways, and get comfortable. The muscle of "adaptation" doesn't get trained, and if the muscle is not being used, it atrophies.

It's not only athletes but any person also who stayed in the same community they grew up in, the same job they got right after school, the same industry they've been in for the past decade, etc.

It requires flexibility of the mind, self-confidence, and psychological energy to withstand the transition conflict.

A person, who changes living arrangements, cultures, schools, jobs etc., is likely to be more flexible and accommodating to change because they have experienced multiple instances of change and have acquired the skill of transitioning from old to new.

After the Podium

People who haven't experienced much change in their lives often possess a much more rigid psyche and have difficulties adapting to new realities.

Strong identification with a profession can be a great building block or a hindering weight.

Let's say a football player transitions from one team to another. He knows he's a quarterback. He also knows what quarterbacks do. He will adjust to a new environment more smoothly in the same role than, let's say, the same quarterback being placed into a banking environment after sports.

A new environment, culture, mentality, and new ways require a mental effort to adapt and change the system to accommodate the person. In the simple example, only a square is available if the system works with squares. If a person comes in and is a circle, they must shape themselves as a square, act as a square, and be a square. Or, as a circle, they can try and make other squares' edges smoother, which is more complex than finding a place where circle systems work with processes where they can integrate themselves smoothly because they know how methods work and how they feel and act.

No matter how inclusive a new environment is, the athlete would still feel lost and out of sync because they no longer know who they are. And their new identity has yet to be formed, and the old one is no longer applicable. The athlete can either restrict themselves to new ways of functioning, which could result in deep dissatisfaction, disappointment, and sorrow, which also holds long-term effects. If the athlete knows who they are, what they stand for and what drives them, they can identify a niche where they fit in perfectly. The problem is that most athletes have always been told who they are and have never engaged in defining themselves or exploring their being.

Many athletes I interviewed reported that their entire life, they've been told what to do, and now suddenly, they have been given the freedom of deciding whom they want to be, a space a lot of them can't fill or handle.

Athletes are so used to taking orders that they don't know or have the experience of exercising their free will. The phenomenon of the athlete is that their willpower is tremendous. They are obsessed with the task. Their self-dedication can't be beaten, yet when it comes to finding a place where they fit, where they can apply their character and talent, they face tremendous difficulty as there is usually someone else who identified their skills' worthiness and character and was able to envision how to use it for optimal results best.

The athlete can have tunnel vision to achieve a goal, yet the athlete rarely sees the bigger picture and how to get there. It is usually a coach or a whole team in charge of obtaining and developing a step-by-step process that the athlete needs to follow and execute. An athlete is an executor, rarely a visionary, a plan developer, or a strategist.

After the Podium

Athletes are brilliant inspirers and role models, yet they're not necessarily the leaders, as the coach is often the leader. The reason why I say that is that the leader is not necessarily the highest performer; the leader is the one who gets his ship to its destination by seeing the direction and vital attributes of every team member and a strategy about using the talents of each player to the best advantage of the whole.

A true leader doesn't have an individual goal.

He is usually unaffected by the ego of being recognized as a leader. He is solely concerned with taking the necessary steps to achieve the best possible result efficiently. We often have our favourites; they are most likely the fastest, strongest, and best. We tend to call them leaders. Because they set a particular record, so this record becomes a landmark to aim for. Yet leaders are usually backstage. What we see is the execution of a perfect plan which we admire, and rightfully so, yet the power behind the vision and strategic plan execution stays out of the spotlight, which is why we praise the work of coaches in the performance of the athlete because of teamwork.

Without the leader's invested interest, the effort put into achieving the result without a strategy in planning can be a waste. A goal is not a vision. A vision is a bigger picture, something that potentially hasn't been done before. It is doubtful to see the leader as an executive in one person because the two are concerned with different tasks. An executive athlete is laser-focused on execution and needs help seeing the bigger picture. It's like a ship; the captain cannot row below as he won't know the boat's direction. He needs to be up above, steering the wheel, analyzing the changing weather, and making necessary decisions, which he wouldn't be able to do if he was to be rowing. The same thing for the rowers; they can be rowing well, with integrity, if they must concern themselves with where the ship is going, how fast or how slow they need to work, who on the team needs a break and who needs to push harder. The rower is concerned with a straightforward task to do their rowing well.

We see leaders amongst athletes who have yet to perform the highest, partially because they were engaged in too many tasks where they rowed and steered the ship. I have observed both individual and team sports. In team sports, for example, leaders are those who would pass the ball in the basketball match to the player who scores higher than them to achieve a mutual goal of winning the game rather than pursuing a personal goal of being seen as the superstar out there, which would potentially put the score of the team in danger and result in the lost game.

The leader can recognize the strongest suits of each player, including themselves, and won't miss the weaker sides to consider all of that when making choices and decisions rather than putting their results first and foremost. Such athletes transition smoothly because they have partially developed vision skills. They have yet to become the highest performing athlete due to their predisposition to their leadership position rather than executive. These are often solo athletes who embark on the journey to pursue their dream of becoming part of a high-performance sport.

This is another reason why transition is hard for athletes. As they enter a new job market, their rowing skills are rarely in demand, so they must acquire new skills which feel like a waste of the skills, like squatting, running, and jumping, which they have been perfecting for the past decade or two. Coaching or teaching is a skill; some naturally possess it, and some don't. Only some athletes can become coaches, even if they remain in their sports and genuinely want to serve and teach.

The transition is always "not yet and no longer." Not yet a banker, baker, entrepreneur etc. and no longer a professional athlete.

The identity is our home base to coordinate and orient ourselves in "space." If I'm an athlete, then I can move to a different country, still being an athlete. I'll find my pack by belonging to certain species. An athlete is my breed. But I keep my part to myself. My role in the group or society is clear to me.

If I am no longer an athlete, who am I, and where do I belong? Even if I don't move towns or countries, I am alone until I find another group or create one where my role is clear again. Our professions are often our identities, as our professions often provide us with the means to survive. It's our barter in the world out there. I feel lost and disoriented if I don't know who I am and what I can do in society. This can lead other people to tell me, who I am, what I should do, and what I'm suitable for, leading to potential employment where I, an athlete, would become just one of many, one of the masses with no definition. It's almost like using the leftover skills "that are good for something." Leftover food is still edible but is not the "first choice" in a restaurant.

As professional athletes, we possess higher-than-average physical abilities. Sure, some of us were born gifted, but many dedicated time, effort, money, and energy toward it. Imagine a child started learning biology in grade 1. By the time they are 25 years old, they already have an advantage; they are more experienced and skilled than any other person who didn't or did very little dedicate attention to this field.

When an average professional athlete retires, they have been in sports for at least 15 years. Here I want to stress that there's a professional athlete and an athlete. A Professional chooses sports as their profession and a way to make their living. Another athlete can still perform high enough but doesn't have to have sports as their primary occupation.

Professional athletes are clearly disadvantaged when they are suddenly measured against the public.

After the Podium

Suddenly 15-20-25 years of experience mean 0 on a job application and a resume.

What if it was reversed? What if our gifted biology genius felt advanced in biology, dedicated his life to it, and was suddenly put into sports or the military? And there was no end to it? Not like, oh, I'll persevere for a couple of years and can go back to my biology, where I feel like a fish in the water. No, not like that. More like you will never be able to enjoy biology to the extent you once did. You wasted your time and energy; what you did, does not matter, and won't serve you anymore.

That's how athletes often feel.

Sometimes, when I talk with someone about this problem outside professional sports, I hear something like, "Oh well, too bad for them; they should've been thinking about it when they were getting into sports and wanted to play all day instead of studying and putting the mental effort into their lives."

These people have yet to walk in athletes' shoes. They don't know because this topic is hushed not only outside of sports but also inside. Because then someone needs to take responsibility for the aftermath effect.

We, as a society, don't understand that athletes are entertainers.

Valeria Tsoy

If we didn't care about the sport, watching it, participating in it, the sport would hardly survive.

If you look at the most popular sports, they are Popular because Population cares. Because sports are a business, athletes are this business's ambassadors.

So, as a society, we also carry a social responsibility for those who work hard for us.

Unfortunately, as every athlete I interviewed admitted, it's not just about getting a job or placement after a sports career.

Germany, for example, offers every athlete a job at the police. They don't have to take it, but it is what they are offered if they don't have other options.

The problem is more profound than just moving workplaces.

The problem is, when one loses their place in society, they are back to being "children" who must figure out how to find their place again.

The thing is, having an athlete as an identity has its security. I look like, "I know my place; I am an athlete in my society. I train, compete, and belong." When athlete leaves sports, not only do they not belong, but they also must figure out where their place is. And as aggressive as our society is sometimes, we rarely make room for someone "new" to come in and take a chunk of our world.

After the Podium

It is a change not only for the athlete but also for the group that the athlete joins. They need to find out who the athlete is. The athlete needs to learn who the group players are. It definitely puts everyone in an uncomfortable position. Usually, when one person joins a group, that person is expected to bend over backwards and fit the existing ways. The group is going to have to adjust itself for more than one person. And so, the search for the perfect fit begins. Before an athlete can even identify a group where they think they would belong, the athlete needs to understand themselves, who they are and what they want/need before they can start the search.

What the majority of athletes do, though, is put the horse before the carriage. They get a "job" or start a business before understanding who they are outside the world of sports.

They know precisely what kind of athlete they are. But they usually need help to clearly portray who they are in society and with themselves.

It has nothing to do with their hobbies or what they like doing. It's more to do with the question of "How can I serve my community?" Mind you; their job doesn't matter at this point that much.

They can be an engineer at a software company and get paid for that, but they can also be a building manager in their apartment building. Making sure the residents are being taken care of. The facility is clean and timely renovated etc. Now he makes money being an engineer, but his service is being the building manager.

Or another scenario. He is an engineer and knows a lot about computers. So, he is the "computer guy" in his community, where people come to him when they need his computer help.

The point is that the service to the "whole" might or might not be the daily job or business. But it is needed in the community/society, and the person can fill in the gap when needed. It can be a volunteering position or a paid one. But it comes from the need and the person willing to fulfill it.

Being able to give is a very fulfilling feeling because it shows that what we've got to offer is needed, which makes us feel accepted and belong. People underestimate the power of volunteer work because our society has become so capitalistic, and money driven. Surprisingly, we can mitigate anxiety by giving and being in service. On the other hand, some people who take/earn/sell more become more anxious.

Here I'm referring again to the research and finding of Melanie Klein and her theory on greed and gratitude.

So, while being on the journey of self-discovery, volunteer work can help with the feeling of belonging and appreciation and open more angles that the person can look at themselves objectively and use to their advantage.

The trick with volunteering is that it needs to be a genuine calling to do that. If it's some bargain or a deal like "Valeria said I'm gonna feel better if I do some service, so I'll go and endure this torture so that I can move on," it won't work. It takes the presence out of the action.

That's different from "I always cared about animals in the local shelter; I have a few hours a week where I think I could help them out and see what happens."

The first approach still is consumer behaviour rather than giving. The second one lets the energy flow in a certain direction. A specific place, industry or service "attracts" or is "calling" you to interact. It shows us that we are full and can give, versus depleted and in need to fill ourselves rather than give.

When I was 19, I went to an ashram in India. When I arrived, they made room for me and my service. At first, they offered to wash the washrooms. I was surprised, and after a few seconds of scanning my reactions, I came back with, "I don't think I can do washrooms, but if you need help in the kitchen, I will gladly be of service." I started with washing kitchen floors and gradually became a sou-chef. My involvement in the community grew, and people became more open with me. I then ended up teaching Kazakh National dances to women after all the work in the kitchen was done. By the time I spent my month at the ashram and was getting ready to leave, I was offered to become a protégé of their guru. Needless to say, I was honoured, yet I had to decline as my sports career had just started to go up. Yet the experience of merging into an unknown community left a profound effect on me.

The experience taught me that through joint work and contribution, people get to know you, and you get to know yourself and others. The more trusting they grow towards you, the more room the community frees up for you voluntarily versus having to claw out some space for yourself. It promotes adaptation of the community, but also its expansion. Expansion needs to happen gradually. The system will collapse if you immediately put a 10-pound baby into the mother's womb. The baby grows slowly, adjusting the organs, the skin, and the muscles gradually.

The law of expansion and adaptation works everywhere. Families, workplaces, communities, and businesses. When a new baby comes to a family with kids, the family needs to adjust and make room. Otherwise, at least one person will feel left out. When a new baby comes, the whole family gets ready to welcome the baby and think about what the baby's part will be. It's not the mother and the father who care for the baby. The whole family is. The mother could be feeding. The father could be taking on walks. The sister might cuddle. The brother might play. But everyone participates. When the baby grows, they make room for the baby to contribute. Put plastic containers away. Put spices in the food when cooking. And so on. Everyone is engaged in the process. And has a time and a place to contribute.

We think we show our children love by doing things for them and delaying their "work" by not engaging them in "chores," but daily participation in the family's tasks bonds the family. When one gets sick, everyone comes together. When one succeeds, everyone gets together. That's what sharing is. Sharing is not giving your last peace away. Sharing is sharing your space and your life with others and allowing them to participate and occupy a part of your life.

People want to be part of other people's lives. That's how they feel connected. But since our relationships became monetized, people have become estranged and aloof. They think the relationship is only to benefit just one side and take away from the other. This also makes them feel lonelier than ever. Our live interaction and communication skill is lacking practice and is now regressing. The more detached people feel the more anxious and aggressive they become.

So, communal participation for retired athletes in transition is one of the most critical steps, especially in the beginning.

There's some ugliness to the truth of professional sports that few want to discuss because maybe professional sports won't be so glorified. Perhaps the influx of parents that want their kids to be professional athletes would decrease tremendously. The kids may not want to go to another football practice to get another concussion, which can turn into schizophrenia. The stadiums may not be so full of spectators if we admit that we are going to the show to see people get hurt for our amusement. Like we did when we were barbarians, going to the Coliseum to watch gladiators get killed.

When we look at our society today, when our lives are much more accessible than it was a few thousands of years ago, we see how much has changed in our culture, how much we have improved in the ways we treat each other, how many social and environmental projects are impacting our world for the better. It's time we do that for sports. Not only inside the organizations but socially too. It's never "their" problems; it's always ours too. We live together; we share this planet and are impacted by one another, whether we admit it or not.

I don't know about you, but I want to live in a thriving and fulfilled society. If not globally, then at least locally. I understand how people around me impact how I feel, think, and live. So do I, and if I affect it negatively, it will only come back to me. So, I want to breed what I want to return to me.

Regarding social responsibility, who bares the most of it? The parents? The coaches? The clubs? The association? The Olympic committee?

What would change if, before a child was to pursue a sport, they were made aware of the side effects, just like the list on the medical labels?

I wonder if parents researched the side effects and looked long-term into what it takes to become the most outstanding athlete of all time if they would continue supporting doping and psychological attacks on their child.

How would the rules of sports change? How conscious would we become of the sports we support and don't?

Many athletes who achieved a lot in sports sacrificed a lot. They often think that after they acquired it all, what a parent or a coach wanted them to, they would be off the hook to do what they wish and catch up on everything they missed. But unfortunately, they can't. Even when they fully retire from their athletic career, and even if they catch up with the majority of what they want to do besides their sport, they run into a few roadblocks.

Number one. It takes time to recognize their wants and needs. There's generally a yearning that doesn't have identification or a name to it.

Number two. They know how to execute a plan but often need to gain the skill of choosing a direction, but also pivoting from one direction to another, and even walking a few steps back after they have already put in so much effort.

Number three. Athletes' bodies are used to particular stress and release rhythms during and after sport. Seasonality plays a significant role in the daily, quarterly, and yearly natural rhythms.

Number Four. An athlete is trying to look for, see and measure results. So, areas of life that can't be measured, for example, love, happiness, connection with their child, friendships, and social circle, start to suffer or are neglected, as they are non-quantifiable.

Number Five. Athletes' bodies change tremendously physiologically. The body was built and trained for a specific movement, which no longer applies. Female athletes who go through pregnancy and give birth are impacted even more.

Nobody is comfortable in the unknown, but people tolerate that state differently.

Another question that should be entering our minds now is determining whether our psychological and objective realities match. It is the criteria of being in the moment and understanding what is happening around us. The athletes scored in this field because they have a phenomenal capability of being in the moment. At least they know this feeling, the sensation of their whole body. The body never lies. The mind can, but the body doesn't.

After the Podium

We, athletes, are control freaks, aren't we? And we have a right to be. It's part of our identity. I'll explain why. Our brain controls how our body moves. As athletes, we've mastered controlling our body, making it do what we want, even if it's tired and in pain. We might experience physical and mental discomfort when we get injured or sick. We are our bodies. We are strongly identified with our bodies and their abilities. Society tells us that the athlete is only as good as her body, and if the body can't perform to a certain standard, the athlete is no good.

Control of anything, body, emotions, feelings, people, and the weather today is precious. Control yearns for instant gratification and the ability to handle discomfort. Paradoxically when the athlete pushes through fatigue and pain, as painful and discomforting as it is, it is also enjoyable and comforting at the same time. We are fit to get addicted to overcoming adversity just because of the neural path in the brain. Our most significant physical and emotional discomfort often results in the greatest pleasure. People, who crave control the most, are usually the most anxious ones.

The vicious cycle continues when athletes retire. And the problem is that the brain craves the same opioids as it used to during the athletic career. Yet, most athletes' obstacles are no longer physical or at least not physically manageable. They feel helpless because they are no longer in control. At least not the control which they once enjoyed. The trick to the enjoyment of overcoming adversity and challenges lies in the body's ability to relax after physical work. The muscle contracts and then relaxes; it's been doing it since the beginning of the sporting career, sometimes for decades.

We would get endorphins after physical work but not after mental work. Many people go on medication and biohacking to relax the mind and body. Yet there is hardly any relaxation as good and effective as physical exercise, especially when the activity is 100% focused. Therefore, sports like tennis, squash, volleyball etc., are much more effective than jogging alone, biking alone, or walking alone because the mind is still engaged in the thinking process, the cycle it was engaged in before to problem solve and make decisions. If you are more inclined to do sports alone, new sports would be great because learning a new sport will require 100% focus and give the mind a break.

Chapter 3

Reality Check

There's a saying, "People are afraid of the truth because it will destroy their illusions."

It says that there are always two realities. One is a psychological reality, in other words, our subjective perception of reality based on our experiences. And a second one is the objective reality, a reality or fact that we have right now in front of us without an emotional decoration.

Most of the time, we are living in a psychological reality.

The more significant the difference between psychological reality and objective reality, the more defence mechanism we develop to keep us from seeing objective reality. The more critical the gap, the more complex and painful it is for the mind to acknowledge the objective reality.

When a person is entirely out of touch and projects wishful thinking or an illusion onto objective reality, we can call it a psychological sickness.

For example, we have a dedicated athlete whose biggest dream is to get on a podium of a specific race or qualify for the Olympics.

It's now been over 15 years that he's been putting his sports career first, sacrificing the rest of his life, working only part-time, so he can train for the rest of the day. He makes just enough money to afford a basic minimalistic living. He jumps from one job to another, obsessed with his athletic goal.

He's getting older, and the body starts to feel the wear and tear of excess training. Friends encouraged him to continue doing his sport recreationally rather than professionally. Yet, he believes his breakthrough is just around the corner. He might even start thinking that his former team is against him, conspiring against his competition participation because they don't like him or are afraid that he will finally win and prove them all wrong.

This athlete will inevitably become very sad, upset, or angry. He will feel psychological pain when objective reality knocks on his door by showing that this dream of his might never come true. It's time to let go and look around for other opportunities. Ideally, in this case, he would ask himself, "Where do I lie to myself, and what is it that I don't see or refuse to see? The point is that changing objective reality is far more complex than changing our perception of it. Yet, trying to fit objective reality into our illusion is far less scary. People use multiple methods to try and change their objective reality. We now have ongoing training and master classes.

After the Podium

Coaches and gurus tell us to push more, do 10x and be "unstoppable." This type of approach might yield some achieved goals. The hard way. Because usually, such tunnel vision doesn't allow a person to see easy opportunities, fast ways, rather than through "sweat and grind." We are more prone to change the circumstances or environment or even people rather than change our perception of it/them.

When an athlete joins a new team, they often carry on an image from a previous team into their new one. A retired athlete hired into a company to become part of a sales team will likely project her sports carer's communication style and other personality traits. Depending on how rigid her mind is, she will probably make little to no adjustments to her new environment. Where subconsciously she is going to be looking for similar traits in people, she was able to recognize in teammates to "understand" and apply skills of dealing and working with those traits. It's like using a stencil or a template of a behaviour.

Depending on her communication or interaction style, she tries to make sense of her new environment and look for recognizable clues. For example, a person's walk reminds her of her former teammate. She used to have a strained relationship with them, without consciously knowing why she started disliking this person who only resembles her former teammate by how she walks. Still, our athlete already fits her into a box that says, "not a friend."

Our athlete unconsciously starts behaving toward her co-worker in a way that would provoke particular behaviour from the other person. Because this is the only way for her to feel comfortable or be in the "known."

Don't we all love the "I knew it" moment?

After all, the transition of how it was and how it became, how it was versus now, never happened. So, our athlete is still living in the past and her rigid representation of self and reality. The problem is that the mind says, "I know for a fact that she is mean, and I dislike her." And that might have even been true about our athlete's former teammate. She could've had a valid point. A slight resemblance makes the mind jump to conclusions about the other person, though. It puts them into the same bucket as the experiences with people in the past. It doesn't look at the person broader, noticing differences. It's like saying that if I see blue, it means it's the sky. So, everything blue is the sky.

This still is our mind's economy, applying what we already have vs learning new ways. Applying already cemented behaviour is easier for our brain than learning to accept other people's faults, emotions, and lifestyles.

It is much more difficult for athletes because of the "tedious mental work" we discussed at the beginning.

This part of the mind is not flexible and strong enough in many athletes. We often withdraw them from the mental work exercise (which school could provide), precisely the cognitive flexibility when it comes to being absorbent, rather than stonewalling the distraction from the outside.

An inflexible mind either doesn't notice what doesn't fit into the "template," or if it does start to see, becomes very uncomfortable. What doesn't fit in creates friction and frustration, which can waste significant mental energy on changing the circumnutates or a person or blocking the "distortion," which brings discomfort.

The reason is that our psyche takes comfort in the known and being right rather than the unknown and uncontrollable. The mind resists transition or a change in representation because it is afraid to lose its imaginary stability and knowledge about things and people, about ways to interact with something new.

Our neural path in the brain almost gets cemented into our thinking, acting, and feeling. The skill of adapting or adjusting is merrily a new neural path in our brain. Imagine an athlete who spent the past 20 years in a sport setting where routines were developed and cemented. Established patterns require much less energy than new ways. And we remember that the human brain always looks for the easiest way.

Valeria Tsoy

The stronger and more flexible our mind is, the easier we adjust to the new environment and the faster we transition.

Depending on how the athlete grew up and how accurate their perception of themselves is will also affect the transition. Imagine this. An athlete grew up in a setting where only winners deserve respect and losers are unnoticed or bullied. They would retire with a representation of themselves as either deserving or undeserving. And their life choices will reflect that.

Let's say an athlete didn't have a good relationship with a referee who was a jerk; it resulted in the athlete losing points and placing low in a competition. The competition was so important to him that his psyche registered this episode as a microtrauma. It essentially broke his affective block. His tension was rising (emotions before the competition).

He competed and was supposed to win and enjoy the relaxation part. Still, the referee withheld that enjoyment from him. He never got to release and relax. Next time an athlete participates in a bid for, let's say, a construction after he has retired from sports, he's getting ready for the bid. The tension is rising. He submits the bid. The athlete starts worrying, what if the compliance committee rejects her bid? The mind starts playing a scenario from the past of the referee and competition. The rejection matches the thinking frame of "I knew this was going to happen." The fact of the refusal fits the frame.

Behaviour like that is usually called pessimism by the general public. Few people understand that the athlete is falling into a broken affective block loop. The only release he might get from this situation is if he actually gets rejected. The enjoyment from expectation matching the reality is very hard to beat, even though the expectation harms the person. It provides relief, and the anxiousness that creates the tension subsides until a similar situation arises again.

It is bizarre, we understand. The best-case scenario would have been for the bid to have been accepted. Yet, it is more important for the mind to release the tension than to be happy. Because being suitable for the psyche means stability, predictability, and reliance, it is a foundation upon which it can rely in situations of the unknown. In this case, rejection is better than the unknown and the potential for acceptance.

Few people are comfortable being in the unknown. In fact, nobody is comfortable in the unknown, but people have different tolerance for that state.

Another question is whether our psychological reality and objective reality match. It is the criteria of being in the moment and understanding what is happening around us.

Chapter 4

Affective Blocks

The word "affective" comes from the word "affect" or tension. You might have heard the expression "he was under the affect." That's when the brain shuts down and acts on instinct or automatic responses.

An effective block is a part of our psyche that forms during the first year of our lives. A regular or standard affective block has three stages:

1. Psychological tension/Discomfort

2. Release of tension / eliminating discomfort

3. Comfort/Satisfaction

4. Pause

After the Podium

Affective blocks graph (Athletes can watch a video on affective blocks in their Residence Profile)

When we experience discomfort, it signals our brain to find a way to release the tension we experience from pain. Pain can be physical or mental. It is also the mechanism that affects our choice in dealing with internal aggression. The stronger the discomfort, the quicker our brain makes us jump to action. That's why so many people prefer to act than wait out or "observe" the situation because waiting or observing creates higher tension in the psyche, which one may or may not be able to endure.

This is also why Athletes tend to be perceived as more aggressive than the general public. It often prompts athletes to get into fistfights, as this response to danger/frustration/discomfort is the only one the brain knows. This is one of the ways to fuel athletic performance.

Fear is one of the main feelings that creates tension in our psyche. That's why we usually act faster when we are scared. The more frightened we are, the more we want to release the tension, to run away from it.

Constant tension wears out our nervous system. When fear is unbearable, our psyche develops a defence mechanism that works for this fear, so the pressure doesn't rise too high and our nervous system collapses.

Yet, if the defence mechanism wasn't efficient, it might send us into a panic attack.

Suppose you talk with someone who has experienced a panic attack. In that case, the person will refer to feelings of rapid heartbeat, shortness of breath, thoughts that they are dying, suffocating sensations etc. Panic = fear. Fear = tension. Usually, unidentified fear would drive a person into a panic attack; we cannot present the brain with a solution because we don't know the source of fear/anxiety.

All we know is that the mind is scared of something. Suppose we know that the brain is afraid of that shadow behind a car and thinks it is a shadow of a tiger praying on us. In that case, we could show that it is a harmless kitten behind the vehicle, and it is just the angle of the sun that makes the shadow so big. Yet, if the brain never finds out what is behind the car, it will continue to fear it.

When we are hungry, we can go on with our tasks without running for food immediately. But if we've been hungry for 10 hours, our discomfort is very different from the original first hour of being hungry. With tension (discomfort/anxiety), we lose concentration.

We also waste energy, and that's when people become chronically tired or get diagnosed with thyroid dysfunction or fatigue.

Of course, adrenaline overload does that to you!

In the end, the body is tired of being afraid.

Going back to the discomfort of hunger.

We are hungry, and the tension rises. We don't eat; the pressure continues to increase. It's like the boiling kettle on the stove. We were hungry… hungry…. Hungry…. and finally had dinner. What happens next? Comfort. We are content. Relaxed. Life is good. We are full and somewhat lazy, enjoying ourselves.

The sequence repeats.

The same thing happens with other discomforts. Now if every discomfort ends with comfort, we grow to be optimists. "Every time I was hungry, the food always came. I didn't die of starvation". This sequence has convinced our brain that every discomfort is just a phase between two comforts. This will be a robust belief system that no matter how bad things are at the moment, in the end, everything is going to be okay.

It's our belief system mechanism. A neural path in the brain, where an event has been repeated the same way a multitude of times, the same trail in the brain establishes a clearer path and certain predictability of events and their outcomes.

For example, if an athlete made mistakes in the first part of the run and ended up placing well overall. That happened 10-20-30 times. They would believe that they will still place well even if they make a mistake. This also allows them to tolerate the mistake better and worry less about it, knowing that the outcome will satisfy them. This is what allows us to have a piece of mind. This is the best-case scenario and a healthy affective block.

Let's see what happens when things pan out a different way. Consider the same example with the food.

The baby just got hungry. Just started making sounds, clenched her fist and made body movements. She's not crying yet, but the mother can already tell that the baby is experiencing discomfort. What does she do? We all know that mothers want babies to be comfortable and happy. Especially if it's a super mom, she knows every sound of her baby, every wink of her eye, every movement of her finger. So, she is an awesome mom because she can spot discomfort and eliminate it immediately. That's what super moms are there for, right?

Let's see what happens for the baby's sake when super mom eliminates discomfort immediately.

After the Podium

When the receiving stage comes too soon, and the amplitude of discomfort doesn't rise, we cannot gain satisfaction. It also disables us from training the muscle to experience discomfort. Discomfort tolerance is our base for teaching skills like perseverance, resilience, and patience.

Let's say we eat until we are full every hour or the minute, we start getting hungry.

How much pleasure are we gaining from eating compared to the food we eat after starving for seven hours? How tasty is the first apple compared to the tenth apple?

Also, note that if we are used to satisfying our needs instantly, how do we feel when it takes time for things to happen? This is our patience work. How much worth will every medal hold when an athlete gets used to winning after the competition? And here's the central question: if the enjoyment is not there, how much effort will the athlete put into training to achieve the receiving part of the affective block that is not all that pleasurable? How many miles are we prepared to walk for our favourite meal versus the one we don't care about?

Let's look at another scenario.

The baby is hungry. The discomfort is rising… rising…rising, and the food still doesn't come... For whatever reason, food didn't come. Something happened with the mother. She ran out of formula unexpectedly, or whatever happened. The discomfort extends for too long.

Imagine an athlete who is working hard to have her perfect technique accomplished. She's trying… trying… trying… on a hundredth attempt, she finally can do it. But it is that time when she's already angry, tired, and annoyed. Instead of delight, she might experience relief or even indifference because maybe it took too long. She had already missed the opportunity to be selected for the primary team. By the time she did it, nobody was watching anymore, so she couldn't prove that she had done it and could have joined the selected team.

It's like needing a tool when the car broke down and somebody bringing you the tool when the vehicle has already been towed away.

After the Podium

Our last scenario is the third type of broken effective blocks.

A baby was hungry, got fed, and now she's ready to relax and stretch. When the mother, father, or any other caregiver picks her up and starts teaching her how to walk, crawl, or whatever, that promotes effort instead of relaxation.

Imagine you reached a new level of mastery in your sport, or better yet, you just became the first person ever to do it. You just dove into the "high" of the accomplishment and satisfaction with yourself, and 10 minutes later, somebody comes and says that somebody else just did an improved version of yours. You got to try and beat them again.

Or you won a competition, and you are celebrating. You get an announcement that a mistake was made, and the other person wins. The interference into the phase of comfort breaks the effective block.

Valeria Tsoy

The natural law is" what contracts has to relax."

So do our muscles, and so does our mind. If a muscle is always tense, it cannot be flexible. If your muscle is strained for too long, it becomes tired and overworked.

Use the same example with the spring. It's physics.

We all have healthy, effective blocks. The simplest one is our breathing. After every exhale comes an inhale. While walking, our muscles contract and, extend, relax. We all have broken effective blocks too. The balance between the two or rather proportions make us either optimists or pessimists. A flexible or an inflexible person, adaptive or not.

We can manage to stress well with 80% healthy, effective blocks. And what we consider stressful will vary as well. Some may stress out that their child is 30 minutes late. They already called the police and have reported their child being kidnapped. Some will lose $1 million in a deal and say, "shit happens. Let's make another million bucks"

Chapter 5

Connected.

It is interesting to know that we all have healthy affective blocks and broken ones, no matter how easy or hard our life path has been. They're all different, depending on the situation. This is also how our belief system works and our worldview forms.

In 1975 Dr. Edward Tronick, an American developmental psychologist, performed an experiment called "still face." It is an experiment in which a baby and a mother interact, but the mother doesn't show any emotions in response to the baby. Her face is still.

The experiment lasts for three minutes while the baby tries to get a reaction from the mother. The infant gets very uncomfortable and eventually, after a few more attempts, completely withdraws from the mother. It is one of the experiments demonstrating the importance of emotional interaction in connection with mental health and human brain development.

The need for feedback is very prominent in athletes. Whether they are looking to fulfill the need from their childhood or have developed this need throughout their sports career is irrelevant. Chances are that athletes would feel very uncomfortable in a "remote" work setting, where they would be expected to self-organize and self-manage. Because sports are a very social environment, asking a mature athlete to switch to a "caved" work environment would require even more effort for transition, which will stress mental well-being.

We're returning to our affective blocks. The lack of emotional connection creates a psychological tension that the athlete was unaware of, then he suddenly gets sick and immediately receives attention and care. The tension is released, and the psyche becomes content.

It quickly figures out how to get what it needs. The release of tension happens by drawing attention to sickness, injury etc. This is when we might get an Athlete, who would get sick or injured more frequently than usual if this is the connection method of the psyche, which developed early on, and at that moment, they often require more attention from the coach or feel that they receive less attention from him or her than the other athletes.

The process is unconscious, and the athlete might actually get ill without "faking it" and showing symptoms.

Another situation could be when the athlete was noticed only when she performed extraordinarily. She only got the recognition of her efforts by both or one of the parents when the result was outstanding. Not only was it always a motivation for extra effort, but also her worthiness and "enoughness" scale by which she was measured, and she measured herself. This kind of athlete would be tough on herself and very likely to be depressed when she cannot maintain the frequency of resources necessary for the connection.

Internet Psychologists called it "the need for love." I see it differently. I've also been taught that connection lets a person feel alive and noticed. When we get abnormal behaviour from people, whether it is just being extremely loud in a restaurant or a suicide attempt in a public place, we can assume that these people have a deep-rooted need to be noticed and feel like they are part of society in one way or the other.

Standing on the podium, announcements can often be an attempt to be noticed and connected. And naturally, if this became the connection style when it comes to transition from sports, this can become a real hurdle, as it would take quite some time for the athlete to achieve as extraordinary results in other pursuits as in sports.

Companies love hiring high-achieving athletes for that very reason. The athlete will be highly dissatisfied until he reaches extraordinary results in the new career in an attempt to be noticed by the upper management and rewarded with praise. Often, such athletes are hired into sales positions in the financial or healthcare sectors. Cutthroat industries give a perfect opportunity for driven athletes to work overtime and make sacrifices. They are competitive and disciplined, without any staff training and a manager, who would need to kick their butt for motivation since the athletes are often self-motivated.

Athletes with an "extraordinary results" connection style will always be self-motivated, hard-working and think about themselves last and the results first because they identify with results. "I am the results I achieve." Extraordinary results mean "I am extraordinary, and I am worthy."

It will hardly make the athlete happy or fulfilled. For these athletes, the critical question is, "Who's approval am I looking for?" If the drive to perform comes externally, there's a very high chance that the athlete is looking to re-establish a habitual pattern.

Growing up, we depend on our caregivers for our well-being. Everyone's well-being image is different. In a family of thieves, their well-being relies on their skill to steal and not be caught. In a family of scientists, their well-being depends on studying and understanding convoluted formulas, so schooling holds quite the value in this scenario.

A child who grew up in a family of thieves knows only one way of living and one particular belief system. Mainly stealing is OK. They will also put very little value on schooling because the school will contradict the parent's authority to condone theft.

After the Podium

In our evolution, our biggest fear is to lose a sense of belonging. This fear is there in every race on every continent. The child can only belong in the family of thieves if it plays by the rules and holds the same belief system.

Teaching established by a German psychotherapist, Bert Hellinger, called "family constellation" or "systemic constellation," explains the phenomenon of belonging through the concept of a family, where an entire family line or family tree is a system. The idea of good and evil is tough to dismiss for an average person based on morality and societal norms, so the system steps out of the cultural perception and aims at just getting to the cause and effect.

Bert Hellinger does just that. A family is a system with working mechanisms and patterns developed over time. For example, a particular watch has a tool. It only works with a specific type of springs, bolts, and screws. Using a screw would damage the watch, so the system automatically kicks the wrong piece out. Does it make that piece terrible just because it didn't fit? No, it doesn't. It just means that it doesn't fit (belong) into that specific watch or system, and we need to find where the screw will fit and find the right place to do what it does best.

Same thing with the human body. If we perform surgery on a person who needs a kidney transplant and put a heart in place of a kidney, even if it's the best heart, the healthiest, the strongest etc., it will be the wrong organ. Every organ has its place and function. A

Valeria Tsoy

kidney secretes urine, and the heart separates the blood in different directions. The body will reject anything that doesn't fall into place. Humans rely on our knowledge of good and evil for critical judgment, yet the system, nature, and a bigger consciousness is smarter than any human brain.

However, when we grow up, we often need help to fully separate between what we've been taught and what we know, and that's when we face indecisiveness and a sense of lost direction. It's like constantly being at a crossroads. And that sense can tear the cycle apart. Because no matter which way we go, we're unable to feel happy. There are two ways to live in this case. Neither is right nor wrong, but one will definitely make us happy. One way is to stay with the traditional way, which often will look like this. Every new generation is a new wrestling generation in a family of wrestlers. And in a family of doctors, every new generation becomes a doctor. The question is, is it really our calling? If so, we're lucky because, as experience shows, most commonly, the family will face a clash of generations, their values, and their way of living.

Contact, whether internal or external, at least makes us feel uneasy and nervous. It's like when you were given the seed of an oak tree, and you're trying to grow a palm tree out of it or at least make it look like a palm tree.

It is essential to understand that we are unable to fight evolution. And evolution, simply put, is survival. Each family generation survives the best they can with the patterns they established for themselves. To put things in perspective, consider some bloodlines that discontinued their existence. It means that the ones alive today are more potent bloodlines for a reason, no matter how society perceives them.

For nature, life is a priority.

Suppose we step away from morality for a second and look at the universe's natural laws. In that case, the universe is a system that self-organizes. I won't go too much into the ways of nature. If I may, I suggest a great movie called "The biggest little farm." It's a movie I give students to watch at the beginning of our study. It gives a great perspective on natural systems' self-organization and the mind-blowing synchronicity of a billion living parts acting as one.

When we grow up, we often blame others, most likely parents, for how things turned out. Unfortunately, with the blame, we also give away our strength. We say they are in control of our lives, not us. That's true until we are about 18 when we're all considered grown-up, employable, and independent from our parents.

With independence, we gain responsibilities and freedom in our lives and ways. The tricky part for most people is that they think of freedom as rebelling and doing everything they have been prohibited from doing or limited from. However, this is only partially true for a simple reason.

Valeria Tsoy

When we rebel and do things out of spite, we often still hold the person or belief as a base. For example, if I had been pressured or at least expected to be a swimmer, I'd quit my swimming career and become a basketball player instead. Or if my mom was always a housewife, and I am a female athlete, I would go out of my way not to do anything with being a housewife.

Either way, we still depend on the expectation or our family's routine as we take it as a standard or a starting point for our decision. Suppose my parents didn't care whether I would be a swimmer or not. Swimming would only be my interest if it was valuable and had a point of attention in my family or closest surroundings. That's how brands, especially the luxury ones, work. It is the value we assign to objects.

Remember, earlier on, we discussed being in contact or being connected as one of the most sought-after feelings. People tend to call it love. I'd instead call it to care when a person cares about what the other one does, whether in a negative or in a positive aspect of it.

When children rebel, they often want a reaction from a parent, teacher or whomever they rebel against. Same thing with athletes and any other person. Won't you agree that it feels terrible when you make something for someone, and they don't care? A child would paint a picture and bring it to her mother. She would smile and say something like "Well done" or "How beautiful." Connect. And so, the child and mother would have these connections throughout the day.

For a child, this means what they do matters, at least to the mother or caregiver. When a child is out of contact or a connection, she often looks for a different way to connect. Or at least see that what she does matters.

And so, she might throw a tantrum, break things on purpose, or do something that would validate that the parent or caregiver still cares. That they are noticed that they exist.

Depending on the style of connecting through childhood, when we lack social connection, we refrain from the type we used to connect with our parents.

Athletes whose parents only praised extraordinary results and fulfilled expectations habitually try to predict expectations. They will match it even if it is to their disadvantage and harm. So, we strive to fulfil the expectations of others, our fans, or our sponsors.

We also don't get as much satisfaction or gratitude when we win a medal because reaching a goal someone else set for us is just a means of connecting. Athletes often find that the standards they once were taught as pillars of happiness don't bring them joy or satisfaction.

Of course, often times it's also a projection of power. Because for a child, a family is a whole world. The saying "it takes a village to raise a child" is very accurate. Yes, it takes a village to raise a child because that child would see different ways of connecting with the world outside. It also increases the chances of getting enough "clicks" of contact to feel I am OK, I am normal, and I belong. I am safe. The more variety of interactions the child is exposed to, the more she can choose from, and the broader the worldview and the colour palette.

For athletes, however, this can become problematic if their life is limited to just family, team, and coaches, especially if that environment is all sports oriented. They usually don't get a perspective of the world outside of sports, which is why it's so shocking when they discover it after retirement. Cultural shock, some might call it.

Travel is crucial for children and adults, so we can see how it can be done differently in different cultures. The problem is when people travel, they often take their culture with them and try to measure the new location against their habitual environment or stay within the comfort zone of being tourists and customers, where friction is avoided for an enjoyable time while visiting.

When an athlete who grew up primarily in a sports setting retires, the transition becomes very intense, sometimes experienced as a near-death experience and a total collapse. Especially if their only way was to connect through their physical abilities by showing results at a training session or a competition; in that case, they experience a psychological death of identity.

After the Podium

An athlete recognized only for hard work will treat every new endeavour, a job, as the next most challenging thing. Instead of choosing something easy or at least spotting accessible opportunities, it becomes impossible for such things to happen easily because it has no value to the athlete. It's almost like this athlete is addicted to hardships because they feel connected and belong by working hard. So hard-working people are looking for hard-working people so each can be connected and become a part of the same club of hard-working people.

People who get it easy, get lucky and don't work hard don't get accepted to the "hard-working club" because they don't fit in and contradict the worth of "achieving the hard way."

It is again a self-organizing system, where some belong, and some don't, and neither is good or bad. They either possess attributes necessary for the system to work smoothly or not. The story's moral is not to change ourselves to fit the system but to find the system where we fit in and where we belong by default. Now, if that were our golden ticket, the world would be a happy place, and since we're not, let's dig deeper into why finding your system is not enough.

Because of one simple reason, we don't know who we are, so we can't fit in. Suppose all I knew was that I was a tennis player and represented as an athlete. When I retire, my transition will be Armageddon because my psyche will go through trauma and all accompanying stages of a trauma—denial, search, helplessness, acceptance, or grieving/mourning and moving on.

When studying the process of athletes' retirement, I looked at the change in the psychological representation, a switch in identity and essentially the effects of losing the identity before finding a new one.

I concluded that the athlete is going through the stages of grieving, which is very close to grieving and mourning a loss of a loved one.

John Bowlby has done much work in this field.

In the best-case scenario, it would take an athlete a whole year to go through the process. I am still trying to figure out the worst-case scenario, but I have seen athletes still going through the process even after a decade of being retired from sports. In the denial stage, the athlete often continues to train as hard as they used to in sports even after they retire. Their body would live through the same schedule and rhythms, depending on the sport.

They would feel emotionally involved with the team or the sport, and those emotions will not necessarily be pleasant. When they gradually merge into searching, they see the faces of their teammates or their coaches on the streets or in shopping malls. They might recognize or look for the car or a bus they were driven in. They might think about what they would do in a sport setting at the gym or recreational sports. In other words, the mind, for the sake of it, would still be looking for ways how to remain in the sport.

The danger of transition is that the sport became their life for many athletes. It became the reason to live, to wake up in the morning, to train etc. It became, by far, the biggest motivation for anything. Demonstrative goals and milestone achievement give the athlete a purpose. When an athlete retires, the purpose of their whole life is crumbling down, and we can say he's going through one of the most painful psychological experiences in the athlete's life.

The discomfort the psyche is going through could well be called a psychological death. During the denial phase, the mind builds up a defence mechanism that would allow the objective reality of the end of the sports career to slowly sink in. It would allow it to drop by drop go through a controlled fence. And somewhere around three months, given an athlete's psyche is healthy enough, the entire volume of new reality would be absorbed. This process and time are vital for the survival and mental health of the athlete. Otherwise, it can collapse, and the athlete might develop a psychological disorder.

In the first stage of the transition of **denial**, the athlete might still be holding on to the potential of what "would've" happened if they stayed longer. If they didn't retire, didn't get injured, didn't get kicked out of the team etc. In their mind, they are still living in the past reality avoiding the present moment and the pain it might bring. The mind is afraid of the pain. Ideally, this stage lasts about three months.

The **search phase**, another 2 to 3 months, is where the athlete might recognize the music they usually hear at the competitions, smells, people, and vibe. They can sometimes catch themselves strategizing about the competition, although there isn't one. For example, they might also notice that their body is acting the same way as it used to in response to seasonality.

Just like I mentioned earlier, there is a point of no return for athletes' motivation. When practices and competitions "out of love for the sport" become a goal with external validation and purpose, they will lose something precious, namely the natural drive and inspiration. And that's why being driven by inspiration is more powerful and healthy. A result and competition against other teams cause athletes to go without doping. Willpower, in this case, can only last so long. The inspiration and internal motivation, on the other hand, are bottomless. We can't skip this phase, and we can't control it either. The best thing we can do is embrace that it will happen and not resist. But it is easier said than done.

Some athletes get stuck in this phase. When they get a job and, let's say, the manager, resemblances the former coach almost mirror. The athlete will resist change until the very last moment because she finds comfort in the likeness. It will apply the exact interaction mechanisms it has developed throughout its athletic career.

You have probably already guessed that when we are stuck in the search phase, we subconsciously seek a work environment and relationships that will copy our previous experiences as much as possible. This is the comfort zone. That's when I suggest that athletes, I work with take at least one year off.

A year where they allow themselves not to choose a new career, job, or purpose. Having enough savings in the bank and time, how to say essential and the body overall to go through the transition process more gently. Those who came to me after working in the field outside of sports for several years usually change occupations afterwards, having to go through a double transition. One is athletic, and the other one is in a new career. Whether the athlete has already planned their after-sports journey, it is essential to understand the biological and chemical processes in the brain during that stage. No matter how much planning and detail went into a future career and life after sports. You'd be surprised that athletic transition can result in heart disease and even heart attack, depending on how fiercely the mind fights change. Of course, it usually happens when the athlete does not know what is happening to them. They try to explain or pinpoint a problem logically. They typically see it in other people and look for the root cause in the current situation and people rather than their past and cemented ways of living.

This is why it is essential not to sugar-coat the transition process for athletes. Their expectations must be that it will be a process of at least a year. It most likely will be heavy emotionally and mentally. They might get moody and sad at times. But all these things are normal and shouldn't be pushed away. On the contrary, only allowing these things to emerge and be seen and felt will provide for a smooth transition as smooth as it can be. Fighting these natural processes will only extend the transition and its phases, which might be painful.

Indeed, depending on how the athlete grew up and how accurate their perception of themselves will affect the transition. For example, an athlete who grew up in a setting where only winners deserved respect, and losers were either unnoticed or bullied would retire with a representation of themselves as either deserving or undeserving. And their life choices will reflect that.

Here is another example.

An athlete ran into a referee who was a jerk. The athlete's competition was utterly destroyed because of that person who didn't like her. The competition was so super important to her that this episode was registered by our psyche as a microtrauma. Essentially it broke her affective block or reinforced the already broken one. Her tension was rising, and her emotions before the competition, she competed. She was supposed to win and enjoy the relaxation part. Still, the referee withheld that enjoyment from her. so, the psyche never got to release and relax. Next time an athlete who has already retired after sports is participating in a bid for construction. She's getting ready for the submission.

After the Podium

The tension is rising, she is submitting the proposal, and her psyche recognizes the pattern from before. The athlete starts worrying, what if the compliance commission rejects her bid? The worry that it might reject, the rejection which matches the thinking frame of "I knew this was gonna happen." The release of the denial matches the structure and the expectation.

The psyche starts looking for a customized traumatic situation from the past. The athlete begins thinking or saying, "I think they are going to reject it. I don't think they like us. This is taking too long; they must have found something in papers they don't like".

Behaviour like that is usually called pessimism by the general public. Few people understand that the athlete is falling into a broken affective block loop. She might only get a release from this situation if they rejected the bid. The enjoyment from expectation matching the reality is very hard to beat, even though the expectation is negative towards the person. Yet it does provide relief, and the anxiousness that creates the tension subsides for a while until a similar situation arises.

It is bizarre, we understand; the best-case scenario would have been if their bid had been accepted. Yet, it is more important for the psyche to release the tension than to be happy. Because being right for the sake of it means stability, predictability, and reliance. It is a foundation upon which it can rely in a situation of the unknown.

Valeria Tsoy

When an athlete, especially in extreme sports, let's say a Formula One racer, the stakes of life are high because a mistake can cost them life. So, when a racer drives 200 km an hour, he is not thinking of politics at that moment or a fight he had a week before with his girlfriend. He is present in the moment and sees where others are, what turn is coming up, and when he stops for a pitstop.

Or a volleyball player, for example. She's not thinking about her dog being sick at home, or her break up, although both can be pretty disturbing. During the game, she's on the field. Her eyes are scanning the situation and are glued to the ball. The list of examples can only go on for a while. To understand their reality at this very moment, all athletes need to do is draw themselves back into their bodies and remember how it feels with their bodies, not their minds.

We need to understand that reality can be different. It can be better than our Illusion or worse. Of course, the majority wants it to be better, but it is often worse. We need to be brave enough to face it and not run away from it or shield ourselves from it anymore. When we need to accept objective reality, we transition to the next stage, helplessness.

In the **helplessness phase**, athletes might feel retirement blues or depression. This phase lasts around 4 to 6 months. Athletes can learn a new skill of living in the after sports world. The reason why we feel helpless is that nothing we know is applicable. This is the "I can't do like I used to and don't have new skills yet." Some athletes fight the stage by setting new goals and achieving them or trying to catch up on everything they missed out on when they sacrificed it for the sport.

Based on my experience, these athletes are gentler on themselves and those around them. In contrast, athletes with external validation motivation are often not only extremely hard on themselves but demand the same, if not higher, standards of others. For them, it needs to be more comprehensive. Why would anyone put in less effort than themselves, work not as hard or have not as high a work ethic as them? Depending on an individual case and overall environment, athletes like that either end up in a toxic work environment or create one for themselves.

Such athletes don't know when enough is enough. Depending on the employer's ethics, he would sometimes hold our athlete back. The employer knows this former athlete relies on them for permission to take a break and regulate the workload. If an employer is not ethical and doesn't care about the long-term results of such work, they would encourage the selflessness of the athlete for their greedy reasons. It eventually results in a "dead horse," a.k.a. Burnout. A depressed athlete who goes through an episode like that or two either quits or gets a medical condition. The feeling of "not being enough" will eat her alive.

Many athletes now look for a job or a business in a completely different industry. They embark on a journey of looking for life's purpose and re-discovering themselves, thinking the problem is in the industry or the company rather than the approach. Such athletes long for a "coach" that would direct them, give them instant feedback, and generally have a close relationship with them.

At this stage, they must face the transition process after sports. A part of their life they have been trying to avoid this entire time. For some, it can be not a year or two later, but even ten years later, when they give up the resistance and face the inevitable. Just because the athlete refused to go through the transition and willingly believed the lie that the mind was telling them that everything was fine does not mean that the process resolved itself on its own. On the contrary, it was lingering and brewing in that far back corner that she continued to push it into. Many athletes suddenly wonder why they start feeling low energy after a few years of post-sports life. Their immune system is no longer robust. Their sleep is a whole big topic for discussion. Suddenly, the world is crashing down; some might even pick up cardiovascular disease.

We need immense psychological strength and energy to push away this whole process.

Imagine it's like a giant black monster staring at you 24/7. Concentrating on things you're doing takes much effort, not to pay attention to the beast but to the task at hand. The monster is waiting. It doesn't sleep, it never leaves, and it doesn't give you a break. It is terrifying. And it's there all the time.

Eventually, the athlete's psyche collapses from exhaustion and gives up control. At first, we might see physical symptoms of tiredness and Burnout, and only later might we discover psychological fatigue, often described as adrenal fatigue.

As we know, adrenal glands are responsible for adrenaline production. A hormone responsible for our fight or flight reflects in our survival mechanism. When the psyche constantly guards us against the black monster of transition, it has no break or relaxation at any point. It is costly afraid. So, the adrenal gland continues to produce adrenaline, resulting from ongoing work and affecting our well-being and, most of all, our sleep. For the body to rest, it needs to relax and be able to repair.

When the psyche acts as if it is constantly under attack and needs to defend and protect itself because it is at war, the body is mobilized a hundred percent of the time.

Our psyche also has another exciting mechanism. It is easier to die, collapse, and shut down certain parts of us responsible for our interaction with the world and things that excite us or make us happy. When it can't bear the tension of fear anymore, it slows down or numbs our emotional system and brain centre not to feel it anymore. The result is the inability to taste life and be grateful for small things childlike.

Valeria Tsoy

If we fear emotional pain, we cannot selectively shut down the receptors of emotional interaction with the world.

Like when we fear pain in love, we limit our ability to experience love truly. Any area of life with a fear of pain we cannot bear will eventually become numb.

The sad part is that we're shutting down our lives because some cannot face fears. That's when life becomes mundane, stagnant, and gray, where nothing exciting says anymore, and there's no point in living. You might have guessed it. At this point, some athletes become suicidal, often because they still remember how colourful and eventful life used to be in sports and what it has become. Some might even try drugs and new experiences until they try at all or become drug or alcohol addicts. Pretty sad, isn't it? Our glorified world of humans is not so gentle on our souls.

The good thing about it is that there is a way out. One that doesn't require medication or hours of meditation in the Himalayan mountains. Our first step is to recognize that the transition for every athlete is a normal and natural evolution of being an athlete. It doesn't mean that athletes stop being athletes. It means they are evolving to a new stage, and the transition is always painful.

Our second step is to educate athletes early on what transition is. What feelings are expected?

After the Podium

And most importantly, feeling these feelings doesn't mean that they are weak or that society thinks they are anything less because of it. Transition for the athlete is a new birth, and instead of tearing it and fearing it, we need to celebrate it and dive into it. The more the athletes resist the transition, the harder it is for the athlete and the people around them. When talking about an athlete's transition, we are talking about a Transition of an entire family or a group.

Often closest people cannot recognize the athlete at all. Athletes have also reported that their life feels empty, dull, or boring after sports.

The reason is that with the upcoming competition, the athlete feels a purpose to train hard to eat well, rest etc., to keep many things in check. It feels, and often also is, that much stuff is going on, and mind and body are involved and busy. But it's an "excellent busy" and purposeful busy. Honouring busy. When the athlete retires, especially in the first year, they can start feeling like there's nothing much going on. So often, they would begin creating action around them, not just for themselves. It creates an illusion that things are the same, if not better, because now they can do whatever they want and have freedom. Yet the majority must determine what to do with their space and freedom. Our society believes that with hard work and dedication, anything is possible. Athletes are no exception, especially those who achieved much in sports with hard work and dedication.

Valeria Tsoy

Every athlete I interviewed publicly or privately admitted that the first project they attempted after retirement failed.

Many athletes also realized that choosing a new direction and passion was extremely difficult. For some, it is still a work in progress.

It is difficult because athletes might need more education, not because they are tired or need more willpower. Because for a lot of them, their direction was already chosen by their parents, teachers, coaches etc. They have never really set the arrival point for themselves. If it's an Olympic sport, society has already established points of interest, such as the Olympic Competition or Olympic champion.

If the sport is outside the Olympic list, it's another tournament that defines success. The athletes doing their sport mostly because they were striving to demonstrate success and keep their place under the sun struggled most. We also need to remember that athletes are used to being physically and mentally active. When the levels of activity dropped, Athletes experienced psychological and physiological frustration. What is frustration? In a few words, it is a space where something used to exist before. Even if it only did exist in our minds, it still holds a spot in our perception.

For example, many people have a confident expectation of a situation, and the reality doesn't match the expectation. We often become uncomfortable, some milder than others.

Still, we start experiencing anger, disappointment, and sadness in the spectrum of other negative emotions. Let's say I left my house expecting no traffic on my way because there is never traffic at this time. After all, I checked an app that told me there weren't any delays, but I ran into a massive traffic jam, which threw me off balance. Depending on the significance of my expectation, my frustration (an empty spot in reality that did not get filled appropriately) will elicit an emotional response to that discomfort. It will be proportionate to the significance of my expectation.

Therefore, athletes rush into action after sports. They are not aware that they are ill. Their body is experiencing emptiness, where there used to be activity, meaning and impact, the purpose of that action. So naturally, athletes try to fill the void with other actions and objects to experience temporary relief.

We are addicted to how things used to be, so we try to keep it that way. Or at least pretend that it is still the same. We create illusions of fullness to avoid the immense feeling that it's not there anymore. The athlete needs to be emotionally prepared for the transition. If they retire in six months, they slowly start the transitioning process. It can be as simple as starting to think about it. Let's implement a few new routines more suited for non-athletes versus athletes. Athletes rush into the action of jobs and education. It is extremely difficult for athletes who have ended their careers abruptly.

I'll show you an example of a pregnant woman. Suppose she mentally did not immerse herself into experiencing pregnancy. In that case, she lives in the same rhythm. She does things like she doesn't have a baby in her tummy. Works until she is in labour. Then when the baby is born, she suddenly wakes up. She became a mother overnight. Even though technically, she had at least 7 to 9 months to prepare herself emotionally for being a mother and having a baby.

These mothers, by the way, are more prone to postpartum depression than those who, hopefully, experience their pregnancy and dedicate at least their thoughts towards being a mother. Unsurprisingly, female athletes often rush into motherhood right after their sports career.

Of course, there's the problem with rushing into motherhood. Athletes who yet haven't needed to undergo the transition after sports go through a double shift. Their psychological representation change is not only from competitive athletes to retired athletes. It is also a competitive athlete, who is not pregnant, who has no kids, becoming a woman who is pregnant or has a newborn. We must understand that the routines, such as sleep, physical and intellectual activity, social activity, and a whole other list of everyday life routines, suddenly change. Nothing is "normal" anymore. And instead of learning how to adapt to a new environment, the majority of people, not only athletes, tend to fight the change and continue living as if no additional variables were added to their lives.

Mainly, an athlete is used to being in control, at least in control of themselves and their body. Unexpectedly everything changes when the baby is here. And that bundle of joy controls when we sleep, eat, sit, or walk. In such cases, many athletes try to fit the baby into their "normal" lifestyle. Some might even take their month-old babies to business meetings, travel with the same frequency etc.

Now there is a baby in her life, her sleep schedule is different, and her whole day is different. At some point, when the athlete supermom burns out or collapses into postpartum depression, she might attempt one more thing. It is to run away, meaning "I should find a nanny or a relative who will perform all the duties that don't fit into the normal lifestyle of a new mother." Of course, this doesn't happen only to athletes- mothers. It can happen to any mother. For the athlete mother, the process is aggravated if motherhood happens shortly after sports retirement, and she doesn't cope well with the transition.

By the way, parenting can affect athlete fathers just as much. Male athletes might feel the same way. Fortunately, when discussing affective blocks and going through a traumatic experience, we generally talk about all genders. Another culprit our psyche throws at us and why so many athletes rush into parenting is the same frustration or emptiness our athletes experience when no more life projects are on the line. So often, athletes take up parenting as a new life project and attempt to climb the Olympics of parenting. We start seeing helicopter mothers and overcontrolling fathers compete with other super parents. They compete on whose child walks earlier, runs faster, and starts reading before they are three. Who gets the cutest lunchbox and the healthiest grass-fed or vegan fresh snacks and lunches?

Much too often, it is not necessarily 100% about the child. It is about the parent. They compete with other parents but also identify with the child. Every success, failure, mistake, and milestone become part of the parent. In this case, such parents often limit and control these children. These children don't have a right to their mistakes. Their super parents or super parent already preplans their life experience. They often need to be made aware of what they are doing. The justification is usually something like this. "I am acting with my child's best interest in mind because I lived longer. I won't let them make mistakes that I have made. Overall, I know better".

The super parents often give themselves another chance at changing past outcomes. Unfortunately, children, in this case, become a tool for achieving the desired outcome through their children's lives, who didn't have a choice to choose a direction on their own. These children compete early in different sports, just like their parents did. Parents coach them or closely supervise the training process with the other coach.

After the Podium

Children are often made to believe that the sport is their passion because that's where their parent's passion is. Through the sport, the child feels the connection we spoke about earlier. It becomes a channel through which a child receives the parent's attention and feedback. The child always wants to connect with the people they love or are closest to. They also imprint the values of their parents, which are sports and athletic abilities in the case of a super athlete parent. Children's self-worth is built upon sports achievements that are measurable.

Now we can only imagine what an athlete raised by another athlete who didn't transition well and replaced their sports or sometimes military career with a parenting project will go through. When these kids are made to correct or attempt to change their parent's past outcomes, problems appear.

Problem #1 is that they were never given the freedom to choose their direction in life. Their career. They didn't acquire the skill of making a choice, but also making a choice, considering what's more favourable for them. They didn't learn mastery of listening to themselves because they were never asked, choices were made for them, or they were swayed to a confident decision. And even though they thought it was theirs, it wasn't the muscles of choosing for themselves and not anyone else not trained. No neural parts. No signals in the brain.

Problem #2. These athletes often depend on their parents, even if they reach the highest highs in their careers. And when that parent dies, the athlete is devastated because the primary motivator is gone. They lost the connection with their parent. In this case, the acid goes through a transition in the sport. We often see athletes' results decline because the external motivator is not present, so the psyche is experiencing an evolution of emptiness but grieving the loss of a parent. The transition of having an external motivator in the role of a parent might take time to complete. Athletes will often continue measuring themselves against what my parents would have felt sad in their minds.

The base of their judgement continues to be one of their parents, not Darren. We end up seeing an athlete, retired or active, experiencing an immense inner conflict, where their feelings and thoughts clash with the ones of their parent. It immobilizes the athlete. They start procrastinating and choose inaction. Who has an alarm to decide for themselves? This is when we often see procrastination as a time to kill two birds with one stone. When an athlete no longer enjoys the sport and continues to perform, they might abuse themselves by doing something they no longer want. Yet they do it for someone else.

Athletes are used to working hard long, and the more challenging it gets, the stronger they push. So, when athletes retire, they do things or look for someone to make it hard because only tricky things are worth having. Hence, they overcomplicate things to make sure that their skill of hard work and walking through the walls is not abandoned to no use. They also tend to make a lot of unnecessary body movements because a pause in action is very uncomfortable. Our society is praising proactive versus reactive. Athletes' or athletes' children are always ready to fulfil people's expectations.

Moreover, the better they sit in the box of the expectation, better yet, unspoken expectation, the more successful they feel. It is an entirely different experience if the athlete naturally gravitates toward making others happy or their wishes come true. There's a fine line between people pleasing being part of their character and fulfilling different people's expectations. Fulfilling other people's expectations can be part of their conditioning and adopted behavioural patterns from the environment they grew up in.

The last stage is the stage of **a cherished memory.** In this phase, the athlete accepts the end of the athletic career, but most importantly, they find closure. Here they see things realistically, without the cloudiness of emotions and grief. They can see both sides of the coin and recognize all their career's positive and negative effects. Sometimes stories they've remembered before would have a new light shown on them. As a result, athletes would discover new details and even change their minds about their career's "appropriateness," "righteousness," and usefulness.

Their perception of what they had and didn't have will change, allowing them to move on, taking useful and necessary experiences with them on a journey. It will no longer be an extreme view of events.

Athletes will recognize that sports careers will always be a part of who they are, but they won't define them or make up the main chunk of their identity, personality, and culture. It's another piece of "I," which can be called upon whenever necessary but won't be the one to dictate the current or future state of events.

As a memory, the experience of being a professional athlete would be fully "digested" and integrated, accepted by the athlete. Nothing will call the athlete back to "resolve," as the state of cherished memory provides the comfort of accepting the way things are without needing to change anything.

After all, we are only drawn back to past events if we disagree with how things turned out. That way, we are stuck and bound for stagnation. If there are still people, events and circumstances that trigger disagreement, anger, or discomfort, it is safe to assume that the athlete is still holding on to the past and needs more time to let go.

None of the stages happen and resolve themselves at once. Athletes will find themselves working through digesting emotional events gradually.

For example, they might go quicker through the experiences of their competitions than the relationship with the coach.

Competition integration might happen within 9-12 months, whereas integration of the relationship with the coach might take years.

We cannot broadly say that the transition is simultaneously over for all parts of the career as long as the athlete accepts the transition process and recognizes the stages, they find themselves in. They will be less anxious to experience it since they know what to expect and realize that it's a natural way of processing situations that they've put in the back corner of their mind.

We must remember that the mind always looks for a resolution. Otherwise, it cannot move on and is chasing its own tale.

When athlete notices that they find themselves in similar situations repeatedly, it could be a good opportunity to examine the loop of repeating events to see where the resolution lies.

Athletes find themselves burnt out even without a heavy workload often because they are running away from discomfort, which the repeating situation is bound to bring with it. Athletes keep themselves busy, so their mind doesn't notice the rut they are in.

The saying "eat the frog" is quite applicable in this situation. Face it and be done with it instead of postponing the necessary task.

Valeria Tsoy

I don't know about everyone, but in my experience, even personal experience, I can't relax until I do the task that's weighing down on me. If I know that I have to do it anyway, I usually do it as much as I can and then relax with the satisfaction and a breather from the "unavoidable."

Athletes, who decide to avoid the unavoidable, often burn out, using up all the energy they've got, but then looking for ways that will keep up the speed of running away, which often becomes drugs, alcohol, and other addictions, like side hustles, for example.

The stage of cherished memory is accompanied by a feeling of lightness, vigour, and enthusiasm. This stage allows one to look into the bright future and vibrant ambition. Athletes become more energetic and optimistic about their endeavours and regain their self-confidence.

Chapter 6

II Types

In my experience, there are only two types of athletes.

First, the ones who fell in love with the sport and decided to pursue their life's passion. It's about the feel!

Second, those who needed to prove something to themselves or others through high achievement and precise results. You show them, bud!

Let's talk about the first type.

The one who loves their sport.

This one will most likely go through the sports retirement transition easier than the second one. And here's why.

The ones who love their sport are generally exceptionally talented in it. So, the child seeing how easily certain things fall in place will continue to enjoy easy achievements. It is essential to understand that the human brain, especially children, always chooses the more straightforward way unless they are already conditioned to persevere. But naturally, a child, without applied manipulation or motivation, which is still a manipulation or pressure, will choose the most straightforward way presented to him. Children are still very much in touch with their bodies and enjoy the movement and emotions that sport enables them to experience. It could also be that sport is the only area where they feel confident in their abilities, or they prefer movement to long times of sitting down.

If we observe kids of young age, it is standard for them to be restless and constantly moving. It is that energy within them that is responsible for initiation. When kids are asked to suppress this energy and sit quietly in school, they soon become unmotivated. We see an internal motivation to do something (we see it even more often in teenagers today) relatively little today.

The child is likely to need an external motivator to start a project, go on a walk, or simply complete a task. They become adults who need mentors, psychologists, motivators, and managers to achieve things or even complete the task they initiated. Children who fall in love with their sports are already somewhat self-managing. As they look forward to their practice, they can sit through long hours at school, knowing that all this energy will be released after school. They can wait to enjoy it.

These athletes tend to injure themselves less and generally outperform average results of the same age group. That's when we see our young superstars.

After the Podium

They stand out, motivated by their love for the sport rather than fear of failure. This internal motivation stays and protects the athlete's mental health as long as this love for sport becomes their life.

They feel they would play the sport even if no one was watching, nobody was paying them for it, and the results didn't matter. However, only a few "unicorns" can stay connected with their internal motivation, bodies, and love for sports. The rest of us could not withstand the collective unconsciousness, societal pressures, and prejudices.

One of the external factors that can break internal motivation is when timing becomes out of sync. When a young athlete, not mature yet, is rushed to level up. It's a fine line between pushing the limit, promoting progress, and putting the horse before the carriage. Today the need for speed has become an international virus.

The sooner you get the results, the better. The sooner we grow plants, the better. The sooner we deliver parcels, the better. There is no room for patience or even natural cycles anymore. Still, instant gratification acceleration is what occupies our minds today. If they could make women give birth sooner, it would become a trend and even a competition. Depending on the child's age, the pressure and responsibility might age them prematurely, where the psyche has not matured yet to withstand the demands, where the burden of responsibility will make exploration of sports passion into a job. "I want to go train" will become "I have to, or I must go and train." This becomes regular self-abuse.

And what is self-abuse? It is doing what you don't want/can't against your own will and well-being. It is another reason certain employers like hiring former athletes because this process is already in their DNA. To put their needs last and the ones of a club, country, or company first. It is these people who would go to work when they're sick. Will work pregnant until they are in labour. It is these people who are reliable.

If we distinguish the word "reliable," we can see "re"-"liable." This means "I make you or them liable for my responsibilities or comfort."

"She is reliable" means "she won't be late for a meeting; she knows it's important for me."

I am putting liability on her for the task, which is essential to me. She has proven, time and time again, that she will put my interest above her own. I deny my responsibility in securing the possibility of all members being on time by, for example, allowing a 20 min "late window when I booked the meeting room, scheduling the meeting during a low traffic time etc. I expect all members to bend over backwards to satisfy my demand because I cannot do so myself.

Reliability is necessary for war and on the battlefield; it is a dimmed sense of self-care and self-preservation, yet a higher sense of duty and self-sacrifice as a prerequisite. We will discuss this phenomenon in the later chapters, especially during the transition.

When young athlete acts out of love/passion for the sport, they are not only given more mental and physical energy towards it but also very much in tune with their body and its ability. She also adopts a "scientist approach." The curiosity of trying something new, more, or different in their sport. It trains an important skill of self-discovery. Being interested in ourselves and our inner world more than the world on the outside will promote grounding and self-reliance, and the skill of "self-soothing."

Such athletes naturally progress, feeling when the time is right. Transitions happen organically, from one level of their sport to the next. On the other hand, they will stop when the time is not correct or when the body is not ready for this moment because the natural instinct is strong.

Making young athletes do what they don't want or feel comfortable doing will require external motivation. Whether it is fear or praise, both are considered manipulations because we make someone do what they don't want, but we do.

Athletes' habit of external motivation has a high potential of turning into a job they hate but get paid for, essentially self-abuse for money, a.k.a. external motivator. Parents and coaches require quite a bit of self-control to keep their good intentions and motivations intact. It is essential to recognize when an athlete needs encouragement and a reminder of who they are and why they love their sport vs trying to fit them into our vision of what's right and what they need vs what we think they need. They must bring it back to basics when they need a break and room to breathe and collect their thoughts instead of continuing to push.

It is hard for parents and coaches to let the athletes, especially young ones, take the reins into their own hands and decide their future careers. Often, adults with their projections come into the place of the athlete. For example, a father who couldn't pursue their sports career for various reasons can live his dream through his child's eyes. It will be tough for him to recognize that pushing his child in decision-making, even with good intentions, unconsciously forces the athlete to do what the father wants or wishes to have done when he was an athlete.

Instead, the father must let the athlete choose, considering their wants and needs. Lots of rationalization can accompany it, and even logic on the father's side to convince the athlete and himself. Yet it doesn't change the fact of the matter.

And given that parents' authority can be a significant component in an athlete's decision-making, it might lead to persuasion and steering in a specific direction. The best thing a parent or coach can do in such a situation is to remain neutral. And as easy as it may sound, it is more complex. Because to be neutral, we need to realize what our dreams and rationalizations are and be able to shield the athletes from them. Such behaviour towards athletes is ethical and mature and should be the ultimate goal. Once we understand that inflicting our desires and dreams onto an athlete can change the course of their life and cost them a life altogether, it puts a particular responsibility that needs to be assumed.

Ignorance can't be bliss anymore.

Most selfless coaches and parents I've seen have been there for the athlete as a support and help rather than a manager and motivator. Once the relationship turns into a manager/motivator-athlete, the probability of an athlete requiring a manager, or an authority figure, even after a sports career, is much more likely. It can also set them up for failure in business. As to start a business, we need to be able to rely on ourselves and our own judgment.

The athlete is doomed to work under another manager when that opportunity is taken away during a sports career. Someone who will know better, know-how, know what and develops a codependent relationship, similar to Coach/athlete, parent/child. If the athlete is not given enough autonomy, they don't mature. They can fear the future until they find a figure who will provide stability, superiority and predictability and essentially assume the responsivity for the athlete's life. A spouse can also play this role, often resulting in a toxic relationship.

Suppose the athlete doesn't digest, understand, and integrate the relationship model of one in sports. In that case, it will repeat the work and personal relationships pattern with almost 100% certainty, as this model would be the only one, they know and will be used as a stencil for any future interpersonal relationships.

Second type

Let's talk about the second type. These people were born talented with extraordinary physical abilities. They recognize that from an early age. They do follow their path in sports, and they succeed in sports. They are praised for their abilities, yet the motivation differs from the first type of enjoying the process and feeding their curiosity.

In the second type, athletes use their bodies to prove their advantage and superiority through their athletic abilities and competitive achievements. Physical abilities are used as a shield to hide other disadvantages. This applies to both female and male athletes. It is a compensatory mechanism and a defence system against deep pain, influenced by external factors, whether family, community or even religion.

After the Podium

The main difference between the athletes is that they use different fuel types. By fuel, I mean psychological energy.

The first type uses curiosity and enjoyment, and the second uses aggression and pain. Both fuels work equally well. The sensations are different, however. As you can imagine, the fueling style will impact the athlete even after sports, making the transition tunnel and further professional endeavours different for these two types.

It's like having a diesel and a gas motor. Both work. It's just a matter of preferences.

You might wonder if switching fuel types in active athletes is possible.

It is possible, but there's a high chance that the athlete with the second fueling type, once altered, will abruptly leave the sport, even if they are at the peak of their career.

This, of course, will throw a whole system out of whack—the coaches, sponsors, federations etc. Here we ask ourselves whether it is ethical for the athlete or not to persuade them to continue their sports career. With the athlete being prevented from leaving the sport because the stakes are too high and would be manipulated into thinking it's just a temporary setback? Or would the top athlete, making the country proud and the sponsors rich, be allowed to choose their path and calling? Because once the fueling type switches to curiosity and pleasure/enjoyment, it will most likely also change the direction the psychological energy is funnelled towards.

Many athletes throughout their careers recognize at some point that they are being fueled by something kept in the dark. Yet, they are afraid of change and the unknown. Even though their current state doesn't make them happy, they stay in their comfort zone because they've learned how to operate and have developed coping mechanisms.

Another factor that keeps athletes in the painful fueling style is the identification with a significant person, most likely one of the parents. This identification will probably show up in an idealization, where the athlete would want to be just as great as their dad, who used to be a former athlete. Or an athlete will see the parent as a rival, so he would compete with the father's result, trying to outperform the parent. There's no room for enjoyment, only the agony of potential failure.

A heightened sense of responsibility for others, which many sports establishments instil in athletes, can break the fueling type and switch it from "the heart's calling" to the "call of duty," the second fueling type.

Both scenarios are equally possible, even if their relationship with the parent is loving and respectful. These mechanisms are working in the background and are often unnoticed.

After the Podium

The second fueling type experiences higher wear and tear on their body and mind. Because even if we say, "fueling type," it is consuming oneself. Where the energy doesn't get replenished and is only spent.

In the first type, inspiration, enjoyment, and satisfaction of curiosity fuel the effort from outside. Have you noticed that when you do something you enjoy, you don't get tired, versus doing something you drag but must do? Do you employ your willpower to make yourself do it?

The second type of fueling and burning originates at the same source. Aggression and pain make us spend ourselves and our life energy to achieve.

The body and mind are in survival mode constantly. The main difference is the illusion that once we get there, we will be happy, feel accomplished, and be at peace with ourselves. In fact, even if we do get there, these feelings don't last long. The achievement quest becomes a way of living, every time demanding from us one last push, one last strain, one last... Until it really becomes a "last." Whether it is an injury on the field or a heart attack at the office. "Last" is a sign that we spent our last drop of ourselves, and the fuel has been only going out, and nothing was coming in.

The second type usually forces an increased speed. It doesn't allow things to happen organically but applies effort to speed things up.

Valeria Tsoy

The agony, the hiding tiger, and the anxiety make them run on all cylinders with barely any rest.

Their mind usually employs the mindset of "10x effort for 10x results". Dare I say that it doesn't often work that way?

No, it just doesn't work. Period.

Let's go back to doing something for money. An athlete who started with a love for the sport and whose internal fulcrum was broken often stays in sports because it became their job, and they get paid for it.

When results become the measurements of success, it kills the spirit. The process loses its soul and becomes mechanical. When the success and worth of the athlete are measured by results only, internal motivation has no room because the focus of attention is moved from within to the outside.

We often see those athletes when they suddenly need additional resources to perform, sometimes not even better, but just up to their average level. It can start with different supplements and progress to doping. And suppose it wasn't already sad enough. In that case, athletes often have to use anti-depressants because of the intensity they need to push themselves to do something they do not support or agree with. This is when we start seeing athletes get injured more often than average. Self-repression is at its peak.

After the Podium

One of the reasons so many athletes fall prey to mental health challenges is their need for the approval of "the outside source." It can be a parent, coach, the public or anyone else whose opinion is often used to determine their worth. As in competition. Because it temporarily releases the internal tension of the anxiety, whether identified or unidentified. We praise the winners and dismiss the losers. It determines a person's place.

Know your place, as the saying goes. It is easy for the psyche to measure itself against a result because it gets an instant answer of whether the athlete is "good" or "bad." It gives an instant identity, a box one can fit.

As we remember, the human brain takes the easiest route. And in this case, the easiest way to determine one's self-worth is to consider a competition placement. If we win - we are good. If we lose - we are "bad." It's black and white. Nothing complicated. Either way, it gets us the fuel to keep going.

It also relies on the athlete's internal beliefs or thoughts placed in their mind. Every competition becomes a test of reality, where this paradigm can be confirmed or overturned.

If we win, we want to continue being "good" and "worthy." Athletes are only as good as their last result. Fulfilling someone else's expectations becomes second nature for us. According to neurobiology, the neural path we build throughout our lifetime is hard to overturn, especially if we are unaware of our automatic responses and behaviours.

Athletes often determine their self-worth by measuring themselves against a result or a person. Something material or quantifiable. And yet what brings us happiness and a sense of fulfillment is rarely attached to a number. Behind every number or every object is a feeling we are chasing. And feelings or emotions can't be seen or touched.

In his book "Blink" Malcolm Gladwell describes a situation where an ancient statue bought from a private collection by a museum had to undergo multiple inspections before determining its authenticity. One of the world's renowned experts on an ancient sculpture looked at the sculpture and instantly sensed that something was off. She needed help to pinpoint what was off while the facts aligned to prove the statue was authentic. The sale occurred; it was later revealed that the statue was a fraud counter fate at the museum. It took them months to determine that the statue was fake, yet the intuition of the statue expert was proven to be correct.

Malcolm Gladwell explains how the human brain works and how our life experiences can be stored in a certain way. And what we call intuition. So that we instinctively can make decisions based on that sense, which only lasts "a blink of an eye." After that, the logical/rational part of the brain kicks in, and we might be unable to access that blink again or start doubting our judgment. Yet during that blink, we're confident. It impacts the internal fulcrum when we start digging into why, we are sure.

For example, a team manager told athletes that landing was safe when a group of professional freestyle snowboarders went to shoot a video somewhere in Japan in snow powder. The athlete admitted that he had this feeling that it wasn't a good idea, just that specific area, and yet he decided to trust the judgement of a team manager. It resulted in a broken leg and arguably the descent of his athletic career.

The more rigid the sports system, the more dependency it creates on athletes. It will eventually break the stem of intuition, self-reliance, and objective judgment. I would say it breaks the person and their spirit and makes them "compliant" and "standard," aka predictable, aka safe to manage.

Such structures and extreme control might produce highly stable results. Still, it is doubtful that they would consistently deliver the highest marks without burning through talent with lots of collateral damage, as rigid structures promote the second type of fueling, not the first. The first type of fueling requires room to breathe and freedom to experiment and be inconsistent.

When an athlete is not free to act on their senses, they are refused to be taught self-reliance and responsibility. When an athlete relies on a coach, judge, or any other system to provide structure, make decisions and plan, it creates a pathological cycle where someone else is responsible for those life-imperative skills. The person is trained to be co-dependent and rely on someone before acting. This creates many problems, where the athlete will blame someone else for their mistakes and won't be able to own their victories either. Or only own victories and make no use of admitting, studying, and learning from their mistakes.

Their self-esteem will rely on the appraisal of someone else. Since their identity has yet to be established, there won't be an internal anchor and internal authority, a fully matured personality, to rely on. They will always need someone else. Whether a coach, a psychologist, a manager, a "better half," or a doctor, it will need to be someone who will tell them what to do, how they feel, who they are, what direction to take, when to take a break and how to manage their time.

Many sports systems work today, not allowing athletes to mature psychologically, regardless of biological age. This prevents them from being independent and self-sufficient, especially after sports. The danger to such sports systems is that mature people/athletes are not easily manipulated. Yet, immature flocks can easily be swayed in either direction because they are dependent.

Chapter 7

Frozen

Most Athletes are amazing at execution. You give them a goal, a step-by-step plan - consider it done. They don't fret about the hard work. They are self-disciplined and self-motivated. They are very demanding of themselves and others, and most importantly, they are very hard on themselves when it comes to mistakes.

Mistakes are considered sins, and even when they "learn from mistakes," the discomfort it causes, and the frustration accumulated over time make them avoid mistakes at any cost. Of course, the intensity varies from athlete to athlete, yet the motivational system in our brains primarily relies on fear, believe it or not.

Fear, conscious or unconscious, has always been the biggest motivator. Before, it was the fear of death. Today the fear motivation is primarily exploited by marketing. "Only today, the discount for all our products is 50%. Don't miss out. Prices are going up tomorrow". This ad stimulates the person's fear of missing out on a "deal" and manipulates them to act, aka "buy," right now.

It triggers the instinct of "food" (survival security), and back in the day, people ate when food was there because food supplies were inconsistent.

The marketing machine is based on a psychological attack to put a person into a state of fear and then offer a release to that fear.

It is safe to call ads "marketing attacks" or "aggressive manipulation for the person to give their money." It's like stealing, hypnotizing, where the person thinks they have done it themselves, where in fact, they were made to do it under an invisible attack.

Another target is aggravating the existing problem and creating urgency around that problem. Of all the challenges, this one stands explicitly out, flashing red light "emergency" to be solved "NOW," and oh, so conveniently, we already have a solution for you.

Today we get bombarded with psychological attacks everywhere we are. Capital letters, lots of red colour and exclamation marks. It heightens our senses and tenses our whole body. Even if we live happy lives, the marketing machine will make us "want more" and think we don't have enough. Because wanting more creates dissatisfaction, pushing us to start looking for a "cure." It creates motivation to act.

To simplify the explanation, imagine this. Our brains have mostly stayed the same since we lived from hunt to hunt.

After the Podium

When we got hungry, our stomach signalled to our brain, "Hey, buddy, I'm empty. Time to get up and go look for food." Then, humans knew there was a need for food (Problem). I need to get (action) a deer (solution). The hungrier the human, the more eager they were to seek food.

The same thing with commercials. The more "urgent" your "hunger" for the solution to your problem, the faster you are to act on it. And if you cannot buy it, it throws you into agony, where your brain thinks you will die if you don't get it. So, it implies all sorts of tricks. Like coming up with a side hustle that would allow you to save up for the thing you "desperately need." Or get a loan or credit or work longer hours at your job.

Welcome to consumerism, baby, the driver of capitalism.

Depending on what the brain considers the "lively necessity," whether it is relationships, food, clothing, home, looks etc., it will react to specific stressors. The higher the "value" for the person, the more inclined they are to respond to triggers that promise to solve their problem and satisfy their hunger. Whether emotional or physiological hunger is irrelevant, the brain perceives it as the same discomfort it needs to eliminate.

This survival mechanism is still very present in our brains today. The brain is there to solve problems. Period. If we are constantly "reminded" that we have "problems," our brain never rests. It is continuously in the "problem-solving" mode, which depletes the nervous system and triggers cravings for fast carbs because that's what the brain needs to function during stress.

When it comes to athletes, they are even under a higher level of psychological pressure. And before, when the training camp is over, when the competition is over, they could relax and let their parasympathetic system rest and restore. Today every athlete who goes on the phone is exposed to more nervous system stressors through social media.

When the nervous system gets burnt out, we often call it "adrenal fatigue." People usually go to a doctor who prescribes something for the adrenal gland or other supplements for relaxation. This becomes a vicious cycle since the stressor doesn't get eliminated, and we are only treating the symptom.

The immature athlete's psyche is exposed to stressors and psychological motivation too early. Unsurprisingly, many athletes come out of various sports with a "broken psyche," full of coping mechanisms and unable to deal with reality outside of sports. The statistics show that 95% of professional athletes go broke within the first five years of retiring from sports. I couldn't find statistics on alcohol and drug use in retired professional athletes. Yet based on my findings, even Athletes holding the title of world record breakers, Olympic Champions and Major League players fell prey to drug and alcohol abuse during and after their sports careers.

After the Podium

Even though athletes are presented with techniques, meditations, and other tools to promote relaxation, they often need to be more effective. Because no matter how well we massage the body and try to relax the mind, none of these techniques deal with underlying psychological anxieties triggered by "motivation." It can be a motivation during athletic training, an online ad, or a workplace.

Did you know that the #1 motivator for many people at work is the fear of losing their job? And the #1 motivator for athletes is the fear of losing a spot on the team or not making "the final pick"?

The number #1 coping mechanism for athletes to be able to function is "numbing"/freezing their feelings/emotions. Once we freeze the fear, we stop caring altogether. The athlete becomes an indestructible machine that doesn't feel or care and gets "the job done." At some point, this way is easier and the only way to cope, to dull all feelings and emotions.

One basketball coach once said, "You can't be killed if you are already dead." Dead is a good description of how so many athletes feel inside. Dead.

Something that could have happened when fear or pre-competition anxiety occurred, competitors' mind games started getting in the way, so the athlete needed to be tough and tune it all out.

Unfortunately, we are not able to block selected emotions. When you are dead, you don't feel the pain, but you also don't feel the pleasure. We become frozen. Sometimes even facial expressions become frozen unless we need to act, so we get these masks of "happy" people on, and you look into the eyes and see emptiness. It is, again, neither good nor bad. It has become a person's coping mechanism and a way of living. They just did what needed to be done to achieve the results.

However, this way, we lose the taste of life, the colour palette becomes gray, and life becomes mundane. There's an established routine. A day goes by, a month, a year or even a decade, and there's no change, like Groundhog Day. People start getting depressed, and life becomes pointless. Usually, people at this stage start wondering about their life's purpose and the point of living. Some will go on the journey of looking for their destiny. And some will use adrenaline as a defibrillator to make them feel alive again.

Wanna go on a roller coaster ride?

They would suddenly pick up an extreme sports hobby, try out car or bike racing, gambling, or anything that gives heightened excitement. For some, fights at a bar or scandal with a spouse could be the tool. All to "wake up" and function for a bit longer, then return to the "source of excitement" again.

Athletes often fear their feelings because our society labels certain emotions "good" and "bad," desirable and undesirable, and positive and negative. But not only that, once feelings become frozen, it requires some effort to unfreeze them. And that's where real courage needs to come in.

Suppose we don't know how to live through our feelings and emotions. Even if we "unfreeze" them, they can flood our minds with unmanageable feelings. In severe cases, the psyche can collapse into schizophrenia due to the inability to handle painful emotions.

The sad part is that when athletes retire, they retire with the baggage of those frozen emotions. Since most don't possess the skill of feeling unpleasant and hurtful emotions, they continue accumulating the "garbage," hoarding those emotions until they cannot take anymore.

Here we are going to Freudian repetition compulsion or traumatophilia, where we unconsciously repeat the same circumstances. We attempted to work through a situation that wasn't able to get resolved and got pushed into the unconscious. We find ourselves repeating scenarios only to face our greatest fears in an attempt to be able to deal with them and overcome them finally. Which means to live through it, gain an experience, learn from it, integrate it, and never revisit it again, as it no longer scares us.

Athletes, especially those with Introjected depression, would start feeling something negative, wrong, or shameful, which no longer makes them look brave or tough. They stare away because it conflicts with the image or the illusion, they've created for themselves and others to hide their fear.

Too often, people who look the most self-confident are the ones who are scared the most.

Professional athletes who spent ten years in professional sports and more show difficulty remaining in long-lasting romantic relationships. I found two main reasons for that.

1. When a relationship becomes closer, and the "flaws" of both personalities start to show, the athlete begins showing inflexibility in adjusting to their own and partner's needs. They usually use an "escape" as a defence mechanism. First to their imperfections, when they can no longer maintain "a perfect image," and then the discomfort of discovering their partner's imperfections.

2. For a relationship to mature and get strong, it needs a more profound connection, the feeling of safety and trust, which can only be built on sharing mutual vulnerability and acceptance.

Athletes who trained themselves to block feelings and emotions, mastered poker faces, struggle to accept not only their feelings but also the feelings of others.

Digesting an emotion without acting on it or going off the rails is a skill.

We can't control emotions, only suppress them, but we can learn to feel them. The psyche is holding the guard and using immense psychological energy to keep that guard. Because if all the blocked feelings flood the system, it might drown the person, and the exhausted nervous system can collapse. It becomes so energetically "expensive" to stay in the relationship that the athlete feels it is easier to leave than to continue exhausting their energy by remaining in the relationship, using up their fuel.

These athletes report low energy, sleepiness, chronic fatigue while in the relationship, and a boost of energy after a breakup.

They make the wrong conclusion that the partner wasn't for them, it was a toxic relationship or that they are better off single than in a relationship.

Ultimately, we are still dealing with underlying anxieties in the athlete's psyche because it didn't have a chance to mature before being exposed to the pressures of professional sports.

I like the Norwegian approach to youth sports, which doesn't expose young athletes to competition. They only play "for fun" and not for trophies. There's no grading or measuring of athletes. Everyone gets to participate and use their best talents to actively spend time on the team. Notably, Norway has the highest percentage of athletes per capita and one of the highest-performing teams in the world, especially in winter sports. Interestingly, Scandinavian countries are considered less aggressive, while North America, Russia and the Middle East are among the most aggressive.

In Norway, children are not exposed to performance pressure and can develop their talents without identifying with the results.

Young athletes exposed to competition too early often identify themselves with their results. They invest in performance to measure their self-worth and start defaulting to this strategy outside of sports, their next workspace, for example.

Understanding what the athlete identifies with is essential because "high-performance and perseverance" is a generic blanket of the "athlete" brand. It is the attributes that the public and society appoint to athletes. We must ensure that the athletes, especially the young ones, have a wide array of things they can choose from and still belong to the sports world.

For example, they culturally represent their country, so they pay attention to what they talk about and how they dress, as they are the ambassadors of ethnicity, culture, minority etc.

They can also be whistle-blowers. An athlete can voice an existing problem and look for or come up with a diplomatic solution.

They can learn about the club backstage and how the paperwork and the politics work.

With that, they mature within the sport and feel that they contribute in their way, not only through their results.

For example, everyone contributes their share in a family with young children. That way, the child feels that they belong and that what they do matters. They participate in the functioning of the family.

Often, parents would assign "chores" to children. It is not my favourite word; it sounds like a punishment. I'd rather "participation or sharing" better. That, to me, sounds like "being a part of something bigger." Now it doesn't apply to work; it also applies to fun, and everyone gets to participate. We also consider "providing" as part of participation for everyone regardless of age. It can be finding a wild berry in the forest and bringing it to a family pot, advertising fundraisers among their friends or selling wildflower bouquets with friends to contribute.

It is sure more difficult for parents to come up with ideas, help them execute and support the efforts, be there for the frustrations and learning curves etc.

It is the same for the coaches. Being a coach, mentor, teaching and training with care is a huge undertaking. It is challenging for coaches to see these athletes go, some without ever recognizing how much the coach has done. And that would happen more often than you think and could be a very problematic aspect to overcome. Continue to care and continue to invest without expecting anything in return.

It is up to the parents of young athletes to notice such things that the coach does for the athlete and mention them. Draw attention to it and show the athlete how many people participate in their life and success so that the athlete doesn't grow up unattached or "independent." So, they realize they've done great work in becoming "great," but so did people around them. So, they grow an appreciation of the involvement of other people daily. This will raise their desire to participate in the processes, like in other people's lives, businesses, training, and growing up.

When our psyche recognizes how much we've been given without asking anything in return, it draws a vast resource to provide ourselves and actively participate and share. It instantly enhances our daily energy levels. This is a compelling resource and much more rewarding than aggression, which we will cover later in this book. But aggression and the impulse to give are two primary sources of energy, where one will become dominant and dictate athletes' behaviour and relationships.

One takes away and fights for something. The other gives voluntarily and with a flow.

One is destructive and finite, and the other is rewarding and never-ending.

Still, the reality is different from what our psyche sees. We would go through it smoothly or bumpy, depending on how conscious we are about the process. Understanding the process and what is going on can ease the transition. Of course, the grieving part is going to be sensitive. Unfortunately, there's no "fast" way of going through these stages, and no skipping either.

But there are tools to make the process better.

One of them is emotional detoxification.

Detox is a very popular word but is generally used for the physical body. Emotional detox is obviously not about teas, juices, or diets.

Logically, for something to be reduced in amount, first, there has to be a reduced amount of intake. To start getting rid of the toxins, we need to stop consuming toxins.

A good start would be social media, which triggers those emotions we cannot identify and address. We become a warehouse of unpleasant feelings that never get expressed.

But the good news is that there is a reasonably simple way to detox emotionally. To express our emotions ethically towards ourselves and others, we just need to watch a good quality movie or go to a theatre or a musical.

When we enable ourselves to live through the emotion of the characters in the story, the ones that would move our souls and make us cry, laugh and experience all the spectrums.

With that, we are opening the door of a warehouse that's keeping the backlog of everything we refused to feel, weren't allowed to feel, or labelled those feelings bad and unpleasant. But just because we refuse to feel certain emotions and feelings doesn't make them disappear. The unconscious continues to store it.

No wonder people are now at the lowest energy points with all the comfort we created for ourselves. It is because the energy is wasted on keeping the warehouse door shut. And the more overflowing it gets, the more effort it takes to keep it inside.

During their active sports career, athletes could have used it as fuel or used competition as an outlet for all their emotions, mainly painful and aggressive/destructive. The trick here is that a lot of the time, if competition indeed was used as an outlet, then it's just like opening a faucet. The water will flow, but so will all the minerals and microparticles in that water. This means that a lot of unidentified emotions would find an outlet in competition. When athletes retire, they lose their outlet, and unnamed emotions and feelings start piling up exponentially.

After the Podium

Learning to name emotions and distinguish them is also a helpful tool, which will allow for cleaning up the mental space and having them somewhat organized.

If every athlete that thinks they failed in sports knew that without them, the world wouldn't have the winners and wouldn't have the sport altogether, they would instantly regain their self-worth. The athletes who didn't succeed are the base of every sport.

```
        /\
       /GOATs\
      /------\
     / Medals \
    /----------\
   / Didn't win \
  /--------------\
```

The pyramid graph.

Suppose we see that we're all connected and play a role individually and globally. In that case, we see our defined places in the evolution of the sports period. Our individual choices might not affect the entire sport to make a revolution. Still, a collective with identical personal decisions drives progress or regresses office port.

Interestingly, athletes who hold the titles, whether world champions or Olympic champions are convinced that athletes who didn't get any medals have it more manageable. Because they have fewer and lower expectations of themselves after sports, they feel a mountain of pressure to show extraordinary results no matter what they do after they retire from sports. The athletes who haven't gotten results praised by the public are convinced that athletes whom the people admire have it more accessible because they get instant recognition and fame.

As you can see, the grass is always greener. Though, for the most part, no matter the results of the sports, after retirement, both sides are originally unequipped to join a new pack right off the bat. The real action has to happen, which in the best-case scenario, happens after one year. In the worst-case scenario, the athlete can get hung up, and the transition phase for a decade or even longer.

Part of a successful transition is the skill of finding and occupying your "place under the sun," moving from one existing ecosystem with its order into another.

Athletes often need to gain this skill as they occupy a place inside a sports organization and its structure and get comfortable. So, the skill did not get trained as, for the longest time, it wasn't needed.

Any person who stayed in the same community they grew up in, the exact job they got right after school, the same industry they've been in for the past decade etc., will have a hard time moving from one place to another.

It requires flexibility of the mind, self-confidence, and the ability to withstand conflict to transition smoothly. A person who changed living arrangements, cultures, schools, jobs etc., is likely to be more flexible and accommodating to change because they have experienced multiple instances of change and have acquired the skill of transitioning from old to new.

People who haven't experienced much change in their lives possess a much more rigid psyche and have difficulties adapting to new realities.

Strong identification with a profession can be a great building block or a hindering weight. Let's say a football player transitions from one team to another. He knows he's a quarterback. He also knows what quarterbacks do. He will adjust to a new environment more smoothly in the same role. The same quarterback is placed into a banking environment after sports. Unique ecosystems, cultures, mentality, and new ways require a mental effort to adapt and change the system a bit chair accommodate the person. In the simple example, if the system works with squares, only this father's available is a square if a person comes in. They are a circle, and the other half shapes itself as a square and acts as a square is square. As a circle, they can try and make other square edges smoother, which is more complex than finding a place where systems work with circles where they can integrate themselves smoothly because they know how things work, how it feels, and how to act.

No matter how inclusive the new environment is, the athlete would still feel lost and out of sync. Because they no longer know who they are. And your identity still needs to be formed, and the old one is no longer applicable. Athletes can restrict themselves to new ways of functioning, resulting in deep dissatisfaction, disappointment, and sorrow. It will also hold long-term effects. Or if the athlete knows who they are, what they stand for and what drives them, they can identify and niche where they fit in perfectly. The problem is that most athletes have always been told who they are. They have never engaged in the exercise of defining themselves. A lot of athletes I interviewed reported. Still, their entire life, they've been told what to do, and now suddenly, they are given the freedom to decide who they want to be, a freedom many of them can't handle.

Athletes are so used to taking orders and call that they don't know or have the experience of exercising their own free will. Athletes' phenomenon is that their willpower is tremendous. They are obsessed with tasks. Their self-dedication can't be beaten. Yet they face immense difficulty when it comes to finding a place where they fit, where they can apply their character and talent. Usually, someone else identified their skills' worthiness and character and could envision how to use them for optimal results best.

The athlete can have tunnel vision to achieve a goal, yet the athlete rarely sees the bigger picture and how to get there. It is usually a coach or a whole team in charge of obtaining and developing a step-by-step process that the athlete needs to follow and execute.

An Athlete is an executor and rarely a visionary, a plan developer, or a strategist. Athletes are brilliant inspirers and role models. Yet, they're not necessarily the leaders' call, as a lot of the time, the coach is the leader. The reason why I say that is that the leader is not the highest performer. A leader gets this ship to its destination by seeing every team member's direction and vital attributes. They have a strategy about using the talents of each individual player to the best advantage of the whole. The leader is usually unaffected, but the ego of being recognized as the leader is solely concerned with making necessary steps to achieve the best possible result efficiently.

We often have our favourites. You are most likely the fastest, strongest, the best. We tend to call them leaders. Leaders are usually backstage. What we see is the execution of a perfect plan which we admire. Rightfully so, the power behind the vision and strategic plan execution stays out of the spotlight. This is why we praise coaches' work in the athlete's performance due to teamwork.

Without a leader's invested interest, the effort put into achieving the result without a strategy and planning can be a waste. A goal is not a vision. A vision is a bigger picture, something that hasn't been done before. Seeing the leader as an executive in one person is implausible because the two are concerned with different tasks.

A leader who is laser-focused on execution can hardly see the bigger picture. It's like a ship. The captain can row below as he won't need to find out the boat's direction. He needs to be up above, steering the wheel, analyzing the changing weather, and making necessary decisions, which he wouldn't be able to do if he was to be rolling. The same thing for the rowers. They can be rowing well with integrity. They have to concern themselves with where the ship is going, how fast oh how slow they need to paddle, who on the team needs a break and who needs to push harder. The rower is concerned with a straightforward task to do their rowing well.

In fact, we see leaders among athletes who have yet to perform the highest, partially because they were engaged in too many tasks where they rowed and steered the ship. They can be observed both in individual and team sports.

It is no secret that many athletes come out of sports injured and with chronic illnesses. While some countries have better medical systems that allow athletes to maintain or at least ease their health conditions, many athletes still need to be thrown off the conveyor after sports with very little to rely on. Whether it is medical insurance or pension, no "benefits package" is offered to athletes after their sports career ends.

When it ends, it ends, often with an injury that prevents them from continuing their level of performance.

Sports often appeal by their prestige and elite, the brand of the sport. It's that practice in the corporate world, where a high performer gets a "recognition diploma" and no additional pay. Getting recognized and a medal didn't cost the company any money or effort. Yet, the high performer is happy about her moment of fame. When the athlete retires, it feels that the sports medals are worth very little.

However, their legacy is worth it after an athlete's retirement. Their stance on a specific matter stays, even if the athlete didn't reach the highest highs. A vivid example is Terry Fox, a Canadian athlete and cancer research activist, who embarked on a cross-Canada marathon with one of their legs amputated. He didn't finish the race as he died due to complications after the cancer treatment. Yet he made a difference, even though some might consider his unsuccessful attempt to complete the race.

Another athlete, Steve Fonyo, finished the race five years after Terry Fox died. He completed, what Terry Fox couldn't accomplish regarding the tangible outcome of the race, yet the impacts were different. While Fonyo's result is impressive and admirable, it didn't get nearly as much attention as Terry Fox's race.

When an athlete identifies with the result, she will lose her identity the minute someone else beats her result. When an athlete makes professional sports part of her mission, she can always carry it through her entire life. The outcome of her career doesn't matter because her mission is more prominent than one result. For the mission to occur, one needs to know who they are precisely, without relying on anyone else to tell them. Athletes shouldn't be measured by results only. Results pass, and missions and legacies carry forward, often past the athletes' lives.

When the athlete retires from the sport, it is usually not just a change in occupation. It is a change in my entire life. Notably, the longer the athlete has remained in professional sports, the stronger their identity with an athletic career is, and the more challenging the change in psychological representation. The same goes for the level of achievement. Olympic champions will have a more difficult time transitioning than provincial club-level athletes. We also need to consider that Athletes' self-worth and value are often determined by how much money they make during their athletic careers. Because if there is a significant drop in earnings after sports, it would add to the hoops we need to jump to transition smoothly and healthily.

Chapter 8

Who is responsible?

Coaches of athletes up to 17 y.o. are responsible for personal relationships with kids. They help or prevent them from working through psychological maturity and compensate for what the child potentially didn't get in earlier childhood.

A coach is more than just teaching the technique of the sport, strategy and counting reps.

When parents are choosing a coach, they are essentially choosing a co-parent. Especially during the teenage years, athletes and non-athletes look for an "authority" outside their family circle, as they often rebel against their parents. They are looking for a person they can look up to, who'd have their back and will understand them and help them understand themselves.

As parents, we are interviewing the coach to be adequate. We are examining what approaches are used, what worldview he or she possesses, and so much more. Just because some coach has "great results" is an arguable scale to measure someone's performance when directly impacting the child and their psychological maturity. The athlete might show great results based on the measurements of the sport and come out with a broken psyche and body after the sports career is over. Emotional abuse can come in many forms, from gentle manipulation and "motivation" to verbal abuse or threats.

Now I might need to be corrected. Yet countless university study materials on sports psychology, coaching of young athletes etc., need to mention something about early childhood education, formations of the child's brain and the athlete's psyche from a neurobiological standpoint. Stages of brain development at every given age and how these stages can be supported or broken.

It is no surprise that many athletes come out of sports broken. But a lot of athletes reach the highest heights having psychological disorders. They live in agony and paranoia, and the only way to ease the "persecutory anxiety" tension is to keep going, pushing, and running away from their fears.

Whether this fear was aggravated by the coach would be unknown. Yet, a coach with integrity and personal ethics toward the athlete could've lessened that fear. It is possible, though, that if that fear was diminished, it is highly likely, that the athlete would not have achieved the same extraordinary results.

We run much faster if a tiger is chasing us than when we run alone.

A coach can be an influential fatherly or motherly figure for a child who either lost one of the parents or, for whatever reason, didn't get to form a relationship with one. Coaches have way more responsibility for young athletes than just training them for results. Like the teachers in the elementary school, who spend arguably more time with children than parents do, so do coaches. They have this precious little human relying on them to overturn a bad experience of their upbringing or support a great one.

I've seen great coaches with tremendous emotional and professional involvement. I've seen abusive and mentally unstable coaches too. Both produced results that stayed in their field and significantly impacted athletes' lives. Coaches need to be screened for negative psychological tendencies before they are allowed to coach young athletes. Many coaches also need resources like therapists as part of their coaching routine. Often, coaches might encounter situations where an athlete might come for support in a problem. The coach might need to be savvier to go through experiences with athletes themselves, where they need help digesting.

A healthy environment in the team starts with an emotionally healthy coach and staff. I'm sure not every parent can "diagnose" a potential coach on "adequacy," so we need to rely on the clubs and associations to do their due diligence. Now here's a tricky question. Would the club terminate a psychologically unstable coach producing the highest results?

Some will, and some won't. Those who won't especially take responsibility for the repercussion of an unhealthy environment that the athletes are put into. We have greater accountability for the athletes who come out of such a climate, potentially after a decade of emotional and physical abuse.

We must think, at what cost do we achieve results? How ethical and humane it is. I am all for progress and evolution, yet I know we can achieve those in different ways. Maybe slower, but sure, in a more long-lasting way.

We are part of nature and a living organism, and we obey the laws of nature that are still not fully known and understood.

If we were to take an apple tree to harvest apples, the harvest's speed, amount, and frequency would depend on our long-term view. If a farmer only plans to have the tree for about five years, it will feed it pesticides. He would make it grow faster, delivering more apples each harvest and forcing it to harvest every year, vs the natural cycle of every 1 or 2 years. It is expected that after five years, the farmer has squeezed out everything the tree had. It now becomes weak, bares very little fruit, and frankly becomes useless. So, the farmer moves on to the next tree and might even cut the other tree, so it doesn't take up the space and the nutrients from the soil.

On the other hand, if the farmer plans long-term and cares about the tree, he will let it grow and mature. He would allow it to follow natural cycles of harvests. When it takes a year to rest, he won't be "upset" with the tree, so it can deliver a beautiful and lush crop next year.

This metaphor depicts the attitude of coaches and athletes. In this case, it is not necessarily the coach that is presented in the role of a farmer. The athlete can treat himself as a farmer who treats the tree the way the athlete treats their body. Do they let it rest or force it to recover faster, deliver more, etc.?

The plague of instant gratitude has affected everyone, and athletes are no different. If anything, we can often see young athletes, who shoot for the stars, rise high and fast but then burn out just as quickly. The greed for instant results and rewards kills the long-term career that one could've had.

Surprisingly, "the muscle of patience" can be trained. A lot of people mistake patience for self-control or willpower. Patience, however, is the ability to withstand tension (Affective blocks) without self-abuse, without forcing to continue, and without the power to push through. Patience is the ability to coexist with discomfort without waiting/looking for it to end.

Patience is something a lot of athletes are being stripped of. Almost every athlete I interviewed has reported comfort in receiving instant technique feedback from the coach. They perform their sport, a heat, a run, a move and are given instant feedback on it being "right," "wrong," "more," or "less." They don't have to wait to listen to themselves and adjust their "settings" to perfect the mastery of hearing and understanding their body and self. Even if there's no coach, we have timers, scales, weights etc. We can instantly measure ourselves with gadgets, numbers and other metrics and get results.

We are a society of results, finite action, and end goals.

Don't we all love charts, graphs, and scales? It gives us a sense of control and predictability. Our mind takes pleasure and comfort in knowing, yet life and business are unpredictable. Athletes trained to be predictable leave sports and are hit with this wave of unpredictability. Instead of adjusting, learning, and practicing living with the unknown, they often try to find predictability.

This can drive them into a predictable, boring, mundane, and unfulfilling job. They probably won't be happy there, but at least it's predictable, making them somewhat calm. They go to work Monday to Friday, perform the same task, get the same vacation a year etc.

We call it stability.

Athletes who choose this career path would get cemented in the illusion of stability, which would make their psyche very rigid. They will most likely have difficulty adjusting to any changes in their professional or personal life.

That's why it is so important to train the discomfort of patience from an early age. Consult with the young athlete about how they feel and think vs demanding to follow strict instructions and not deviate from the plan. Adjust the body to the schedule vs adjust the strategies to the natural cycles of the body.

This would make the "production of athletes" highly uncomfortable and challenging. The custom environment and approach are the complete opposite of conveyor manufacturing. Yet, if we look at the greatest athletes of all time, we will see that most had custom schedules, private coaches, and approaches.

The conveyor produces average ordinary results, and individual attention produces extraordinary results.

Chapter 9

The Curse of Success

Here we need to address depression that is not easily seen or diagnosed. Sadly, it became a norm. Paradoxically norm is not necessarily the best or at least pleasant. It is the majority. And when most are sick, we consider "sick" a norm.

Let's talk about something called Introjected depression. It is usually a depression of the successful ones. Bizarre, isn't it? I am not saying that every person we deem successful is experiencing this depression, but it is very prominent in athletes. Mainly because athletes directly interact with the masses. Again, we must refer to "the father of spin," Mr. Bernays, to understand how the masses are conditioned. What is expected of the masses is expected by the masses.

We tend to associate specific behaviour when we hear the word depression. Generally, we think of a person as moody, low energy, pessimistic and sad. With introjected depression, things are different. An athlete or a person with such depression wears a success mask.

This depression is also called a "depression of expectations." Suppose these athletes couldn't preserve their internal motivation and love for the sport independently of their results and measured performance. In that case, they start listening to authority in hopes of determining who they are or who they should become.

Athletes are most likely to receive feedback that they must strive to become champions.

First regionally, then nationally, then internationally as a cherry on top. These expectations are first scanned from the closest surrounding, like family, friends, school, coaches, and clubs.

Have you ever noticed how quick people are to give a piece of advice on how a person should live, what dreams to pursue and what career to choose? How many athletes have been groomed to fulfil the highest expectations of their parents? One of the most exemplary cases is Tiger Woods' career as a world-renowned golf player. There's a lot of publicly accessible material on this phenomenal athlete's autobiography. The effect of his ex-military father, who was building an invincible machine within Tiger since early childhood, using warfare tactics, is mind-blowing.

We can witness Woods's hardship after his father passed away. Tiger was going through two transitions at the same time. First of losing his father, and second, of losing authority, the fulcrum, the fundamental base upon which the whole structure was built.

Valeria Tsoy

Self-representation in this depression relies solely on the outside source. Our society praises success and achievement. So, depression has a mask of success, willpower, and invincibility. This depression is experienced solely on the inside. This is why it's called "introjected," originating from the word "intra" in Latin "to the inside."

On the inside, these athletes feel dissatisfied with themselves. They adopt a model of "I am bad. I am not worthy of love." They cannot fully enjoy an achievement, as they always look a bit past it, knowing that this pleasure will not last forever. They are already bracing themselves for the next achievement and accomplishment.

Figure skaters on the Russian national team are conditioned that even if they become world champions today, it means nothing to them tomorrow. Skaters must be ready to prove who they are at their next event. So, the fame and praise last only a day, and afterwards, work begins again.

In my experience, over 90% of athletes showed more than three symptoms of introjected depression.

One of the most prominent symptoms is the "need for speed." In other words, acceleration of delivering high results, progress, and achievement. Unsurprisingly, our society has become mental about instant gratification and measured outcomes. Athletes are subjected to it even more, so their transition after sport is much more dramatic.

Another fear accompanying introjected depression is a fear of criticism in comparison. You can only imagine how much criticism athletes go through regularly. With the rise of social media, it became an avalanche. The fear of comparison is there because it's often a self-comparison, where the athlete never wins. After all, the comparison is not with what's below but with what's better than them. So, self-worth vastness is constantly fed the paradigm that if I'm not good, a.k.a. winner, I am bad, a.k.a. loser. Of course, if there's always something or someone better, there's always a willingness to better ourselves. Look at how many coaches' programs and courses are on the market today. All to better ourselves, relying on internal dissatisfaction about who we are already. How many self-improvements tools, gadgets and techniques are sold to those who need to be more content with who they are and what they can do?

Athletes are measured every day, multiple times a day. From mere reps and sets of physical body performance, two more complex biochemical results of their entire organism. The hook is that this way of living gives a sense of control over what is happening. If the weight on the scale goes up, they can change their nutrition and training, and the weight will go down. If endurance is lowering, supplements or exercise regimens can be altered.

It gives a flawed sensation that everything can be changed, manipulated, and transformed to the liking as long as there is a goal. A mindset of "I see a goal, I see no obstacles" is adopted.

The attitude that anything can be conquered given enough effort and pressure.

That way, the athlete always has a tool called "do more." If they are not satisfied, then go and do more. We'll implement the hacks to get around the defence mechanism if their body breaks down or resists. The biggest fear of an athlete with introjected depression is failing.

When we look at introjected depression and affective blocks, we can see a direct correlation between balance and stress tolerance. For athletes without introjected depression, the anchor or the base is internal, meaning I have myself, my skills, my values, and my knowledge. As long as I have myself, I am fine. I know how to interact with the world around me and understand what I have. A person with introjected depression is almost in a continuous fight-or-flight response. They rarely experience the satisfaction of the receiving part and live through the discomfort because the norm becomes the tension or pressure, a.k.a. discomfort.

It's a painful paradigm where self-improvement comes through a lot of effort. Our society praises sleepless nights, work after hours, and spartan conditions. It praises discomfort, but we need to learn how to be comfortable. The notion of "not enough" is an unhealthy pattern that could have been formed by parents, coaches, teachers, etc. For example, a young athlete enjoys his bronze medal after a competition. A parent throws in something like, "Yeah, well, if you didn't make that mistake, you could've had a gold medal now." Or a coach would say something like, "Only winners are remembered." and that's it. The psyche decides that third place is not enough. Mom, dad, or a coach will only love them if they win or are first, as every child wants to make their parents happy. When we talk about love, we talk more about belonging. It's a human self-preservation instinct to belong because back in the day, we survived together, starting with families, tribes, villages, cities etc.

The human psyche is deeply connected to belonging.

Belonging also means contact. What does it mean to be in touch? To be connected is to know our place in the family, team, and society. It is our self-identification and a sense of belonging. To be connected is to live life together. A mother can love her child profoundly and want the best for him, but she will ultimately be out of touch with the child. So, she put him into the best private school where they taught him engineering early so, he could succeed in life. She forgot to watch and listen to what kind of child was before her. And the child could absolutely love to play piano and become the world's best pianist. Still, the mother knows that pianists are not in demand, yet the engineers are.

Where from an early age, they teach them to figure skate. And even if the child is physically talented, she might not be destined to be a figure skater here. Because parents live longer and are more experienced, they think they know what's better for their child, expressing their engagement in a child's life. Continually raising a successful human being or even an athlete becomes their life's project or their calling and purpose. Unfortunately, these well-meaning parents often need to remember to be in touch, check in with the child, observe them, and consult with them. Usually, this project of raising a champion is because of the parent's project, and the child is put to live a life that someone planned for them but is not necessarily their own life. Often, raising a champion becomes this idea that the parent lives on. And the frame of that idea is very rigid. Everything that falls outside it is neglected or labelled "bad." What doesn't fit will either be forced to change to fit or dismissed as unnecessary or nuanced.

The word idea can fall close to "ideal." And the ideal is based on the idea of what's good or bad, black, and white, worthy, or worthless. This often causes fanatism, whether it's a crusade, which caused deaths around the globe, terrorism in the modern world, which often was in the name of God, or even the second world war, the idea of a perfect race.

An idea demands an execution plan, and someone obsessed with it often justifies specific methods and their consequences. For example, athletes harmed by doping or mental pressure are collateral damage in the name of progress, patriotism, or science. A parent with the same idea of their child becoming the first champion of their race in a specific sport would psychologically manipulate the child into believing it is their dream.

After the Podium

They have to work hard for it. The child might have never thought of such a vision if the thoughts were never placed into their mind. The child relies heavily on a parent to look for direction and problem-solving.

She doesn't have the tools to navigate the world yet, so she depends on the ones her parents provide. In our society's eyes, such athletes and their parents are glorified athletes for their hard work and determination and parents for their dedication and perseverance.

However, if we ask these champions and pioneers if they are actually happy, just a few of them, with a hundred percent frankness, would say, that they are.

Chapter 10

Athletes and Aggression

Aggression in sports is accepted as long as it is within the rules. And then aggression is not necessarily towards anyone. For example, an alpine skier racing down the hill in icy conditions can charge at the gate aggressively and let the emotions out that way. Remember, aggression becomes the unconscious go-to feeling for many athletes to drain the sewage of other underlying emotions, identified or unidentified. These emotions are suppressed and accumulated in periods between competitions. In my experience, this emotional detox mechanism for athletes is unconscious and unknown in most pro sports.

As you can imagine, the body gets addicted to the release and the accompanying feelings. We discussed it briefly earlier in this book. It becomes a trained neural path in the brain. Like Pavlov's dog experiment, the athletic mind has a neural pathway that tries to complete itself. Let's say you are an athlete with a "give it all you've got" attitude. Aggression (in an excellent sporty way) accompanies you your entire career. Through the experience of aggression during the competition, you flush out everything else you've accumulated emotionally, anger, sadness, frustration, and despair. No matter how the game went, you would still feel relieved. Maybe disappointed or joyful, depending on the outcome of the competition. But relieved. Pleasantly tired.

As we remember whether it is a mind of a child or an adult, it is always looking for the easiest and fastest way, and automated methods are always the easiest and fastest. So, aggression and give it all you have attitude become an automatic response to tension and stress even when the athlete retires. It can become a real issue depending on the amplitude of pressure and release the athlete can handle. And the more significant the tension amplitude, the more enjoyable the release would be. Now put it into a real-life situation, that is, warehousing emotions. People around him might even think he is calm or just mildly stressed. Then he suddenly blows up like an atomic bomb when he can no longer stop until he lets it all out.

It can get regrettable. We have seen athletes who would end up in the club or a bar fight resulting in fatalities. And, of course, it doesn't take away their responsibility for their actions. We can clearly see that it is a condition of a psychological affect that often is uncontrollable. Primarily when it was supported and even trained explicitly for decades, it no longer has an application in life after sports.

It is the same with extreme sports and addiction to adrenaline. When athletes retire or can't pursue their extreme sport even recreationally, it is possible that unconsciously they can start creating situations in their life that would make similar biochemical reactions in their brains as the extreme sports they used to pursue. Depending on their underlying fears in life, they'll try different sports or test those fears in different ways for a release. Often it can become gambling. Gambling chips, like they gambled their life. Of course, the solution to this addiction to the "fireworks experience" is a conscious approach.

Once the need for a release through one mechanism is identified, we can build a new highway and find a more ethical neural path. We can start with something as easy as a cold plunge or controlled contrast showers. A cold creates a stressor that mobilizes the body to create an opposing force to balance the extreme, but in a controlled situation that promotes adrenaline response. And after the cold exposure is over, our body is relieved. The adrenaline is no longer present when the stressor disappears, and the body flushes with pleasant feelings through released hormones that are not stopped in a moment, the way we stop a controlled cold exposure.

Mind you, though, that this is also a tool and should be used consciously, or another addiction can be created.

After the Podium

We need to keep in mind that this will take time. It is also part of changing psychological representation; the actual change might start only after six months of consistent progress in the right direction. The six months mark can often be one of the most turbulent times of the whole year, and as long as we are aware of that, we can remain intact with ourselves and be gentle with our minds and body.

In my experience, almost every athlete pursuing change and any new endeavour need to be gentle and in close contact with themselves. The problem with athletes is that they are selfless but harmful. They will bend themselves over backwards if necessary to achieve a goal. There I meant self-control could get in the way of self-care and self-love.

A simple contrast shower must be done in a self-care mindset and a gentle approach to oneself rather than an attack that must be fought through and endured. If I have a terrible day and the last thing, I want is to expose myself to cold water, I won't force myself as I used to in sports because I must or owe it to someone. I might not even do it. After all, I care about myself, and it is my responsibility, not anyone else's.

/ Valeria Tsoy

Chapter 11

Can I?

Our modern culture has become highly phallic regardless of geographical location, culture, and educational levels.

Symbolically phallus is a sign of strength and high potential. Culturally it is a demonstration of our "I CAN." Today success and admirable qualities of a person, especially an athlete, are measured by what a person can or cannot do. Not coincidentally Olympic Games are a symbol of the highest abilities of the human body and the greatest test of its capabilities.

It is also worth noting that women did not participate in the original Olympic Games. The first female athletes competed at the 1900 Olympic Games in Paris. The culture of I CAN is a culture of results. In other words, you can either get it up or you can't. It is factual and obvious.

As men cannot publicly demonstrate their private areas, and women don't have an organ like this, the symbol of "I can" becomes a trophy. A House, a car, jewelry, a watch, and of course, a medal or a globe at the competition. Since women wanted equal rights in the competition of genitalia, a pissing contest is out of the picture. The culture of sports allowed women a way to the stage as well. Women today compete in almost every sports event men do. Women earn money and are placed on Fortune 500 list. Women own real estate and drive fancy cars. They lead big corporations, showing that they can as well.

Notably, in countries where women are suppressed and not allowed to participate in all sports or in specific sports, we can see the roots in men wanting to retain the superiority of the male gender over a female, at least in its material representation.

However, the paradox is that we never ask ourselves why "can we?" We are generally asked why we were unable to. People/athletes hardly ever break down their success to see the building blocks of it. If I ask you, why could I do that? Often the answer will be, "Because I sacrificed my relationships. Because I took drugs that hurt my health and body. Because I pushed through fatigue. Because I suffered through the pain. Because I cheated the rules. Because I lost myself in sports and didn't have a life outside sport etc."

The list can go on, but we avoid asking this one fundamental question at what cost can I/could I do that?

This is also true for sports coaches who fall prey to the cult of "I can." Independently of their own athletic results in the past, they have a new tool in the machine – the athlete. We often see how coaches identify themselves with their team or individual athlete's results. The goal is no longer to support the athlete on their journey ethically. The goal becomes the result, and it changes internally, what should and shouldn't be done, what's ethical and what's not, what is essential and what is not.

The desire to become the best often becomes a life strategy and the fuel to keep moving forward. Now there's nothing wrong with wanting progress. There are two different ways of achieving progress. First to rely on an external source to determine our progress and success. And second, have internal guidance and internal motivation to keep pushing forward.

Athletes generally adhere to a predetermined schedule. Only some would ever have the luxury of choosing to compete or not to compete at an event based on their inner condition. Most will disregard how they feel physically and emotionally during that schedule.

And if not disregarded, then most likely, the athlete and the coaches would put enough effort into promoting change to fit the envisioned "form" that would promise the best performance possible.

For example, the peak form must be in February because the Olympic games are held in February versus the natural rhythm of the athlete being March or October.

After the Podium

It is rare to see the athlete "not feeling it today" act on that inner dialogue and take a chance to say no to a competition. Multiple factors are at play when such a decision is or isn't made. Some of them can be the perceived courage to withstand public shaming. Pressure from the club, coaches, and parents, believing it is their last chance to prove themselves, glorification of self-sacrifice etc.

I have also noticed that reliance on the outside structure of material/logical calculation can force premature "progress" yet can also limit naturally driven acceleration.

Introjected depression has one powerful compensatory mechanism called "I am bad" or "I am not good enough." This mechanism is developed in our prefrontal cortex. A place in our brain responsible for self-control or the "I will, I won't, and I want" motivational part of the brain. There's a great book from Stanford University by Kelly McGonigal called "The Willpower Instinct."

Once the psychological tension of self-worthlessness and endless expectations from the outside and the inside become unbearable, a psyche can survive in only two ways. One is adaptation, and the second is evolution.

It is essential to distinguish the difference between adaptation and evolution.

Valeria Tsoy

I see adaptation as "giving up" and bending backwards to fit a rigid system, which means adapting to the environment and becoming passive. Or active in moulding oneself to fit in.

On the other hand, evolution is fully recognizing the situation one is in and learning new skills to improve an individual's interaction with the world around them.

Let's say a dancer constantly has blisters from any shoes they use to perform their dance. The adaptation would be to get used to the pain and just numb it, suffer through it, and develop a technique to distract themselves during the performance so they don't feel the pain. Evolution would be going to a shoemaker, creating a shoe that bends the way the dancer needs, finding a material with the necessary qualities and even starting to make their own shoes.

Many people, not just athletes, choose another option: to fight and protest the system. It doesn't promote evolution, just destroying an existing system with nothing better to replace it. Yet, feeling helpless and tired of the discomfort they find themselves in, all they can think of is getting rid of it versus evolving in it.

The protest can be passive or active. Both have aggression involved in it. In passive, the aggression is directed inward; in active, the aggression is directed outward. Yet both are a waste of time because, more often than not, it only yields improvement if a person's situation changes, since a new skill/knowledge still needs to be acquired. So, the person will most likely find themselves in a similar situation until they collapse or find a way to evolve.

Interestingly our ability and willingness to learn and evolve are directly correlated with the amount of "available energy" we've got. Thus, tired people are less likely to know if they spend 100% of their available energy on daily activities. How many people nowadays feel like learning or studying at the end of the day? In my experience, people want to study and learn but feel "low energy" to do anything, even if it's fun. When we dive into why they feel so tired when they are not even 40 years old yet, they often resist/protest what's happening at work or in life, whether it is new leadership at work, the new schedule for the kids, a new job for their partner or any other changes happening at once.

They feel tired because they feel comfortable and "wish" for "things to stay as they were." Protesting and Resisting things as they are, they are trying to pull back and keep on doing things "the old (read comfortable) way." So, when people are tired at the end of the day, they pull back instead of accelerating forward. It is like surfing when the wave pushes you forward, and you paddle backwards. In this case, you either learn how to surf the wave, or you keep on living through the "washing machine" experience. Mind you, both ways are energy consuming, but at least learning how to surf is productive, and washing machine is useless.

So, when we find ourselves "too tired to learn," it is most likely due to our wasted energy on resistance.

When an athlete finds themselves resistant or "annoyed" by the change, they must understand that they must find someone to help them learn comfortably. It is like asking to lend them the other person's energy/fuel to get where they need to go to acquire the skill. They need support. And that support can often look like another person, potentially a coach, a parent, a friend, who is just going to be there to say that everything is going to be okay, they can do it, they make progress, they believe in them etc.

In my experience, what helped in those situations the most, was finding someone who already possesses that skill and getting inspired. Mind you, "leading by example" means nothing if people are not inspired by example. They will only be encouraged if the leading person possesses the "spirit." The spirit can be their vision, cause, and belief, but they must live, be, and radiate it. In a sense, this leader is taking the burden of responsibility for "predicting the future." If they truly believe in the direction they are heading into, the change for those who follow them will be less "unknown" and hence less frightening. When people resist, they are not mean or lazy, they are scared, and fear paralyzes them.

In business, a lecturer on business who never built a business and has never gone through the turmoil of daily operations is far less inspiring than a seasoned entrepreneur who walked the talk and lived through the experience.

Which ship would you be inspired to go on? The one whose captain sailed through the storms or who read about those storms and has instructions on what to do if you find yourself in a storm in open waters?

Athletes often gain inspiration from coaches, yet, if the coach is indecisive, it will be hard for the athletes to feed off them and get inspired. A team member can also be an inspiration, yet to inspire; they need a fair amount of freedom in decision-making. If the system within the club, team or federation is too rigid, it will kill the spirit required in order to inspire change.

There are only two ways to motivate people to act: inspiration or fear. In sports and business, motivation with fear has been predominant.

If you don't do this, you will be kicked out of the team. If you don't do that, the sponsors will cancel the contract. If you don't learn, you will be fired. You need to work to get a promotion. Your home will be foreclosed if you don't find a side hustle. The capitalistic machine of "extracting wealth" from the working class has made the general public anxious and hence aggressive.

Valeria Tsoy

We have never lived through a more belligerent society than we have today with all the comfort the modern world offers.

Athletes live through double the anxiety load daily. Pre-competition anxiety is present in every athlete in different proportions. The agony is making them run faster, jump higher and push more. They are then exposed to the mania of the world outside of sports. Their psyche doesn't get a break and is operating on emergency 24/7, especially if the climate inside the team is toxic, where coaches are trying to create additional competition amongst athletes for higher results.

Unsurprisingly, we see an influx of mental and physical breakdowns in athletes. Some medications can delay burnout, which is virtually unavoidable because burnouts happen mentally before they happen physically. The education material has not been updated when it comes to physical loads, and theoretically, with the advance in pharma and technology, we should see the natural abilities of the human body advance and prolong, and yet we see athletes' bodies deteriorate sooner, with the higher impact of wear and tear and inability to build new non-athletic careers after transitioning out of sports.

It is no problem to find a job as an athlete. The athlete's problem is keeping the job and being mentally and physically fit to withstand the job demands. Sometimes they are moderate, but when a car has 500.000km on it, even a 100km ride might be too far.

After the Podium

As some athletes reported, they feel 60 at the age of 30.

60 is a retirement age almost, and we expect athletes to build a new career from the ground up.

I used to get frustrated with young athletes asking me for help finding them a job, and when it came to employment, they would not show up to even interview for a position. It was when I understood what was happening.

It is not just a depression when they "just can't." A combination of their body and psyche breaks down and needs rehab. And yet there's no guarantee that they will fully recover from the collateral damage of a fantastic career.

They are used to constant stimulation. And unfortunately, that stimulation was usually painful. Like whipped to get going, to avoid the pain, they would not stop. The go-to motivation to act becomes avoidance of pain. So, athletes would find themselves in a loop of painful events only to recognize that they put themselves in those situations on purpose because they expect action of themselves when they have no energy to act. One athlete called himself a "sucker for pain." Because every time he felt like his life was slowing down, he looked for the "whip." One time he was gambling his whole inheritance to find himself broke, so he would need to work to build up his wealth again. Another time he invested in a risky business and lost it all again. Next time he married a girl, who took all his money etc. He didn't recognize a pattern until he found himself in an emergency room with severe burnout symptoms and was put in a hospital for two weeks, unable to do anything.

As we discussed in the Introjected Depression, the need for speed is a coping mechanism to run away from anxiety. Every pause is feared, as the anxiety could shorten the distance and potentially close the gap. Facing these fears is deemed unbearable because athletes often don't know what they fear. And as we know, the unknown is the scariest, as we can't prepare for it. Hence, we have no control over it.

Losing control is amongst the top 3 fears athletes face, whether retired or active. When they are active, they feel control over their body, so they work out more. When retired, they feel they have control over their money, so they work more.

When asked what happens if they lose control, they usually say, "I will die."

The fear of losing control impacts their sleep and concentration level, impacting their overall quality of life and the people around them. Their ability to learn a new skill and engage in tedious studying is also impaired unless they turn the fear upside down and think that they are better prepared for what's ahead of them if they know more.

Then it becomes a never-ending marathon of studying, certification, courses, and master classes only to withstand the competition of being alive (aka employed/financially stable). They only compete because of fear. If they were calm inside, there would be no need for the race to the bottom. It's a paradox; calm people work less, are happier, more relaxed and want less. People, who are anxious work more, do more, are less happy, constantly tense and need doping, whether it's coffee, drugs, sex, food, or anything else, that brings a heightened experience of "being alive."

Number one remedy for the "speedy" athletes is rest, something they will never let themselves have unless someone else takes responsibility for it—for example, me. If I "order" an athlete to rest, I take responsibility for what happens, and I am in control and "guarding" them from anxiety. This lets them relax and regain their energy, finding time to drink more water and give up a low-carb, low-fat, low-anything diet. Many people don't see that dieting is a massive mental and physical effort that puts additional stress on the psyche in an emergency mode. Many athletes go on an enforced "hospital regime," which is just taking a break and doing what they would've done if they were put in a hospital. Just not taking it to an extreme and voluntarily eating, sleeping, reading, walking in fresh air etc.

A coach, a parent, or any other "authority" could act as a doctor who can "prescribe" rest to the athlete. It should be an employer too, who sees the athlete burn out, but I rarely see employers who would stop their best-performing employees from working and producing results when no one else is in the company. It is not their responsibility to look after grown-up employees, yet it is in the employer's best interest to keep talent than go through high turnover. It turns out more costly than being humane and ethical.

An adaptation is agreeing to fit the "norm." This way, we need to mould and shape ourselves accordingly to fit in, while evolution is a change that will allow us to go back to whom we were born to be with all our imperfections and strengths and develop a mechanism where our internal and external can be intact with the realities of our modern life.

That could be that the athlete never wanted to be an Olympic champion. His mother wanted it for them because she thought that an Olympic medal would open doors to new opportunities, but the athlete just wanted to perfect his sports skills so he could become a coach for kids. Because he absolutely loves spending time with kids and knows how to speak the same language as them, because he knows how to make complex things fun etc. And he could've already been coaching for a decade now, but instead, he is still chasing the Olympic medal.

And kids, who could've fallen in love with a sport thanks to him, never did and maybe became part of the wrong crowd because there was nothing else to choose from. They could have become a sports team member and, instead, become gang members.

After the Podium

We never know how our choices might impact the lives of so many. In tunnel vision, becoming a sports coach in a small town might not seem such a big life accomplishment, especially compared to an Olympic gold medal. Yet, if we look at the small-town coach who affected crime in the city, and built a school, essentially saving the lives of multiple families, put things in perspective.

Whenever we doubt our choices and inner conflict arises, looking at things from a wider angle is always beneficial. Is winning at the Olympic games or any other big tournament or competition bad? If you noticed, I haven't labelled either sports or striving for perfection, good or bad. I have seen athletes achieve the highest highs in sports but with different motivations. Their motivation was internal. The drive to train more and do more came from the love of sports in general and curiosity about themselves and their sport. They've pushed more, tried more and essentially achieved more, not because their self-worth depended on it, but because they couldn't try it, they envisioned it, or they got an idea.

They became mad scientists in their sports in a good way. Because they try things and see what comes out of it, they are not associating or identifying themselves with an unsuccessful attempt. Making mistakes is part of the process. But curiosity, if I'm interested in what's going to happen if I do XYZ, gives a different type of fuel rather than fear of what if it doesn't work, what if I fail. This gives a whole different range of stress resistance or, better yet, stress absorbances, like amortization in cars or a fork on mountain and dirt bikes.

Chapter 12

Women in Sports

Women in sports are an exciting phenomenon.

First, because competition evolution is considered to be a masculine trait. Even by observing animals, whether today or thousands of years ago. The goal to mate usually triggers competition in animals. A stronger male gets to extend his genes and mate with the female, who is ready for reproduction.

Only a handful of animals females exhibit competing for males. The only other time we observed competition in females is during the fight for survival, which is often for food or territory, like the fight for a lush area, where a female species might exhibit aggression and enter a fight or flight state.

When it comes to humans, female athletes have shown a higher aggression rate compared to non-athletes. It is interesting to note that some studies have shown that aggression levels affect fertility in females.

Evolutionary aggression is linked to reproductive conflict among females, especially of the same kin. Older siblings are likelier to win the battle and have more children than younger siblings. This conflict highly affects sexuality and overall self-esteem. Conflicts arise instinctively versus consciously planned. Fight for dominance is a natural ranking in tribes. That's how order and hierarchy in the tribe are established. There can't be two dominants of the same sex on one territory.

Interestingly, some studies show that a woman can have problems with fertility if her mother is residing with her in the same territory, home, community etc.

Now with aggression in female athletes, the same is true. Where ranking of the tribe and internal hierarchy takes place until the tribe self-organizes and establishes ranking within the group/team, with the most aggressive one likely getting the position of leader. Until a leader shows their status, conflict and chaos will persist. The female leader, who is likely to have a higher sex drive, will then compete against other more aggressive females but now outside the team.

Essentially, the top female athletes are more likely to express higher aggression than those who couldn't reach the top rankings. I assume this because many more components can be at play. For example, doping often involves hormones, which would artificially drive aggressive competitive behaviour through a change in the hormonal balance. A higher sex drive can be sublimated into aggression, which boosts athletes' power and strength.

Soviet Union coaches were well aware of that. And so, they used to get male soccer teams and female gymnasts to go on training camps to the same facility right before the competition. While love was in the air, coaches were vigilant that athletes didn't enter sexual relationships. This way, they ensured that all the build-up was to explode during the competition. Sexual hunger was effective for both men and women and acted as a natural booster of physical and mental performance.

Survival of the fittest was at play. Symbolically, athletes compete for the right to dominate territory, give birth to offspring, and extend their genes.

Essentially This is why competition drives survival mechanisms. It stimulates adrenal secretion and puts the body into a "fight, freeze, or flee response."

Aggressive behaviour in athletes drives high performance and fuels the psyche to push the body beyond safe stress exposure. Depending on how an athlete's sports career turns out, the proportion of wins and losses will often determine the overall self-esteem of the athlete. The experience of being a professional athlete working on achieving the highest performance will be linked to the size of goals the athlete would try to achieve after sports. It will affect their risk tolerance, self-belief, and the feeling of the internal right to belong in society. If a sports career is deemed unsuccessful, the athlete is likely to contain a belief that they don't have what it takes to achieve a successful position, build a thriving profitable business, or climb high on the corporate ladder.

The experience of professional sport is likely to be projected onto the next professional endeavours.

A highly aggressive environment in which female athletes find themselves stimulates the fight or flight response of the body, which is procreation. Sex drive would, in this case, be driven by survival instinct rather than an emotional connection that the female athlete develops with her partner in a relaxed and "safe" time and environment.

We can also assume that this survival instinct response to an aggressive sports environment could cause a higher divorce and break-up rate among athletes after childbirth. Where necessary connections weren't established to promote a long-lasting partnership between the two partners, and once instinctual attraction diminishes, it is difficult for the couple to sustain their unity. Their sexual attraction might reduce within 1-3 years after childbirth. And if the (unconscious) instinct to procreate was the basis for the couple to come together, it would be challenging to find a foundation on which the couple can fall back to withstand the challenges of their relationship.

To understand aggression, often painted as an "unwanted" or "bad" emotion, we must break it down. Aggression essentially is psychological energy that arises in us in response to discomfort. But, if we are uncomfortable, we get a boost of energy to apply to resolve the discomfort. Yet many people, including athletes, often lack the skill to direct aggression toward a productive outcome. Many think that expressed aggression is beaten-up faces and broken noses. But that is not true.

For example, a wise way to use aggression is this. An athlete was fed up with a cable company failing to establish an undisrupted connection and would break down two years in a row during the Super Bowl game. So, frustrated, he got an internship at that cable company to understand how to fix the problem. He then set up the cable tv for his entire neighbourhood and walked away. The company made multiple job offers for him, but he declined. This fact is irrelevant, but I enjoyed this story ending and wanted to share it with you.

It illustrates that through a very productive way of using aggression, an excess of energy is bound to be applied to improve a situation.

Yet, what we mostly see is suppressed aggression or flushed. Suppressed is when we have a frustrating event/situation and decide to do nothing to resolve it. Whether it is a toxic relationship, a loud neighbour, or a harassing boss. But the energy doesn't go away. It stays and accumulates until it reaches a boiling point and blows up, often around people who least deserved it and just became scapegoats.

Then we have flushed frustration, and that is when we find ourselves in a frustrating situation. Still, for whatever reason, we cannot direct it toward the source. It could be if we have differing views on the vision of the company's leader. Contradicting them would mean being fired. Currently, "fired" and "voiced disagreement" are impossible choices for various reasons. So, we recognize that we cannot express ourselves in the work environment. We might go to the gym and punch a bag or embark on CrossFit training. We've used up the energy, feel relieved, and can maintain our calm. Yet we will continue finding ourselves where we need to flush energy because the energy is given to change the situation. Suppose that energy is directed at a workout vs the workplace. In that case, the loop is not broken, and there is no progress or evolution. A solution to that problem could be looking for a different job, understanding the leader's new vision, etc.

Yet, we see the phenomenon of "quite quitting," where people express passive aggression, which can translate into an unwillingness to cooperate, low performance etc. Passive aggression can generally create a very toxic environment not only for the person who is experiencing frustration but also for the people around them. Often, the person can become aggressive toward co-workers because they cannot handle the aggression they are experiencing and are unaware of coping techniques to loosen up the tension.

Female athletes come from an environment where aggression is directed at performance, often even artificially stimulated to get a boost. The body gets used to the "fuel" amount and habitually produces a certain amount of energy. When athletes leave sports, they continue experiencing excess energy (aka aggression) with no skill of identifying the source of frustration and then directing productive aggression towards it vs destructive aggression, for example, in relationships, where instead of looking for solutions, they might get fed up and break up the relationship and still not learn the skill of using aggression productively. It can start with conflicts, where aggression is expressed and flushed through a fight, but no agreement or change is reached.

They might still employ "relaxation techniques," which will allow them to hold on and continue a little longer but won't necessarily improve their relationship or promote any change. The following relationship afterwards will generally result in the same frustrations and levels of aggression. Many people then start avoiding the "stressor" and avoid relationships altogether.

This behaviour is habitual, as many athletes are used to the hierarchy in a team or a club, where they are the soldiers, who execute an order, no questions asked. Even if they don't agree or experience any other frustrating event during their sports career, it all is generalized by the psyche and is used to fuel performance. That is why, no matter the outcome of a competition or a race, an athlete might be disappointed mentally but relieved physically. So, the coping mechanism for many athletes becomes "just to carry on, as it will soon release no matter what." Where they don't understand that in everyday life of a non-athlete, there aren't scheduled "relieve sessions" (aka competitions). That's when athletes might get in the loop of getting into fights regularly just so they can somewhat function normally. Some use drugs and alcohol to suppress the excess energy given to them to evolve and not waste. Same thing with money, by the way.

Recognizing even mild frustration is paramount for athletes, as they tend to get fiery and misplace their excess energy and suffer consequences that can be pretty gloomy.

A woman becomes aggressive when she is afraid. Aggression is given to handle the source of anxiety. She can either fight the source, run away from it or freeze. Freezing emotions is a way to handle fear because fear is exhausting, so it shuts down to give the psyche a break. Before this, fear was stimulated by survival threats. In the modern world, we hardly ever face constant threats like a tiger hiding in a bush or a neighbouring tribe attack. What we face are bills, social media, and marketing machines. If a woman, after childbirth, doesn't feel safe, she cannot relax. If she cannot rest, she is nervous. A nervous mother raises a nervous child. So, if we want to care for our children, we must care for our mothers. An anxious woman will drive anyone nuts at home, work, school, etc. A nervous professional female athlete is double the trouble because they are not afraid to act. But their actions are often irrational because they act in a state of affect (immense tension) without seeing the whole picture clearly.

Yet a relaxed woman can create miracles. A peaceful, grounded woman has no problem with breastfeeding, tending to the child, with creating a home where the family can rest. A woman who fears for her well-being won't be able to do any of that. And as much as it is her own responsibility as an adult to provide for herself when she is in the early stages after childbirth, she finds herself in a very vulnerable position of needing to be calm and relaxed around the child and flex, tense up to "hunt for food."

What goes up must go down. What tenses up must relax. A simple law of physics, the law of balance, equilibrium. Yet, when in a partnership, both partners tense up to provide. They both need to relax. Generally, for a woman, there's no room for relaxation, as with the responsibility to provide, she also inherits the responsibility of parenting, cooking, cleaning, and extracurricular activities of children.

When women started fighting for equal rights with men, mostly for the right to work and equal pay, the lines got blurred between the societal roles of men being providers and women being caretakers.

After the Podium

And I can see both sides, where women were repressed for the longest time and demanded respect. Because in our society, women were disregarded as grown-up individuals and were often patronized by men, which gave men a sense of power and, in some cases, put them in a position of dictatorship. Yet, I also see how women hurt their position in society. Because of demanding equality, they somehow inadvertently demanded: "the right to be a man." This often was triggered by the notion that because women weren't providing or earning money, they were perceived as weak and unworthy.

Our society has become increasingly capitalistic with very materialistic values. The demand for equal pay was also pushed because even when women strived to provide and work, they were often underpaid, which still kept men an advantage. So, no matter what women tried to do, whether earning like men, working like men, debating like men, or knowing like men, they still needed to catch up because women are not men. It's like a kangaroo trying to be a horse and being measured by a horse's success standard. Seems absurd to me. We didn't need to fight men. We just needed to enhance and appreciate women's role in society more.

Very few saw the value in a peaceful home and a happy nourished family. Many women misinterpreted the "equality right." Its essential purpose was to gain equal respect and worth for the contribution of women to society. Women are the ones to praise for a healthy community but are also to blame for the nervous and aggressive society.

It is in women's power to turn things around when it comes to the environment, we live in. Would you rather be around a relaxed worthy woman or a nervous one constantly fighting for her worth in a male way? We can't compare men and women. They naturally have different purposes in this world. No one is more valuable than the other. Because the life of humans won't exist if we exclude and undermine one or the other.

A suppressive regime of religious beliefs towards women also affects how women see themselves and how much aggression they generate in the space around them.

Athletes will get this metaphor for sure. In muscles, we have agonists and antagonists. One muscle group contract and the other lengthens. This creates synergy in the body and provides its effective function. What happens if both muscle groups contract? What happens if both lengthen?

It was a rhetorical question.

We see the balance of opposite powers in almost every naturally created life. We don't perceive one as more important because one needs the other to be useful. Yet, when it comes to humans, somehow, we dismiss this natural state of balance and claim one to be more important than the other. As long as masculine will be perceived better than feminine, or paycheck is more important and peace and calm at home, we won't be able to reach the equilibrium.

So female athletes, who spend at least half their life trying to perform and sometimes outperform the results of men in their field, have to start training their parasympathetic nervous system or the antagonist muscle group, which is responsible for relaxation.

Men wouldn't need to spend this much time trying to relax using different techniques, tools, and gadgets if they had a woman who knew how to relax and take care. French like to say "cherchez la femme." Which means seek the woman.

Women could well be the cause and the effect.

And if we taught women how to care for themselves, we wouldn't need to "make" them care for others. It would come naturally from an internal sense of abundance and overflow.

A woman with dignity, self-worth and self-love cares and nurtures because it is natural to her, not because she must. If she must, then it is unnatural. And what's unnatural creates friction and frustration, resulting in tensions and build-up.

A woman, who comes out of sports, a soldier on a battlefield, rarely knows how to put her needs first. Her needs were never considered. So, when a female athlete is put in a position where she needs to care for someone, like her baby, she treats that task as a job that needs to be done right, or better yet, perfect. It doesn't matter what flows from her naturally, as her just being her. It becomes a project where she needs to find the "best approach," a standard, a manual of "how to take care of a baby."

We all strive to be independent. Feminism is strong on female independence. We can't bear the thought of depending on anyone because it gives that person power and control over us. Yet, we do depend on each other. Animals depend on each other. The whole of nature is interdependent. Everything affects everything.

Women might depend on men to provide, but men depend on women to keep their minds clear, release tension, relax and enjoy life. Women go for their independence through material achievements. Men either "buy" relaxation, whether it's massage, food supplements, or drugs or try to learn meditation, stretching and other bio-hacking technique to replace a woman in their life. Each one of the groups goes in the opposite direction of their natural predisposition.

If you disassociate from the gender, it will be easier to fathom this idea because then your identity is not involved, and you can observe it from the side. This should give a more unbiased look at the situation. Depending on the environment we grew up in, we have a specific "idea" or right, wrong, good, or bad.

After the Podium

If that status is being challenged, the min automatically defends the status quo and put up a wall where we refuse to see thing differently. But we should step away from ourselves and look at an idea neutrally, without categorizing it. In that case, we have a chance to see the real picture.

One of the hardest things for female athletes is to pause. Their workaholism is their ethics. Only working they feel worthy. If they stop, they might feel depressed and unmotivated. Traditionally women have been seen as child bearers and nurturers. Many women protest that designation. And rightfully so. No one wants to be told what to do and who they are. An enforced power vs natural flow will always meet resistance. Many female athletes identify themselves as warriors, and that identity hardly involves a fragile baby by their side. The image of "girls' power," advertised so heavily by the media, forgets to show where all the powers of women lie. If we nurture only a female's warrior side, all she knows is war and fight. Then she is perfect for business, the army, or the workforce. Don't cloud her mind with having to have a baby, cooking tasty dinners, and creating a cozy home that she also "has" to possess to be a respected member of society.

Nowadays, the universal woman's image calls for "business/career, financial independence, supermodel looks, kind and understanding wife, nurturing and always available mother, open-hearted and welcoming friend oh and then a selfless volunteer to the community."

So, in other words, a hermaphrodite. An ideal combination of two opposing forces. Where a man and a woman are 2 in 1. What a great idea! Then we can feel fully independent. Melanie Klein, a British psychoanalytic, dedicated her life to researching the phenomenon of the inability to manage dependency.

American scientists performed an experiment called "Universe 25." The experiment showed that when rats were provided with a comfortable environment: Food and water were supplied, the temperature was warm, and no outside threat was present, the Pack of rats lost their roles in the community and became individualized. They no longer depended on how their fellow rat mate did their job and how well they performed their designated tasks. They became independent. Females became aggressive and refused to mate, and male species became "pretty," spending their day on "beautifying themselves" and showing no interest in fighting with other males for the female species to procreate.

In 600 days, the Pack would go extinct. The experiment was performed 25 times. Each time result was the same – extinction.

Independence is being an adult, yet ethically depending on the world around us. Giving in to natural forces (circumstances) releases us from anxiety. As it doesn't send us into a fight or flight mode, it allows us to interact with the world around us. As simple as me wanting to wear high heels on an icy cold day. I can hate winter, complain about it, and even wear my high heels as a sign of "I can."

After the Podium

Then break my leg and cursed the ice. Or I can move to a place without winter and keep on wearing my high heels. I can wear different shoes and wait for better weather. I can even ask my husband to carry me over the icy patch if I still want to wear those heels. When I don't resist my dependency on circumstances, people, etc., I have many options for interacting and getting a win-win outcome.

Frustration and disagreement to settle down are great traits that can be very productive and serve evolution, individual and communal. Planes, for example. People dreamed of flying. Some complained, and some even "flew out of spite," so to say, and some imagined and built planes.

Our dependency is positive because we must adjust our plans and actions. Our dependency benefits from other people's dreams, stubbornness, and frustrations. Those, who got fed up with a horse and a carriage, created a car. Those who didn't want to do laundry by hand anymore created washing machines. If they didn't get frustrated by certain things and didn't use their aggression, driven by frustration, productively, we would still be cavemen for all I know.

We depend on things beyond us, greater than us, and things we might not know of, but it doesn't mean that we stay unaffected by it.

Chapter 13

Athletic Mothers

Often female athletes would have children right after retirement. And it feels like they have a new purpose of becoming super moms. These moms are putting as much pressure on themselves as they did when preparing for a big competition.

Now the world of moms has become a competition arena. This "super mom" sport is multidimensional and multidisciplined. There are so many awards to win. The healthiest breakfast. The longest breastfed baby. The earliest walker. The fanciest lunchbox.

Social media sets the goals for the moms themselves. Moms no longer must set goals; society will do it for them, and supermom athletes will achieve them no matter what. They'll attempt to reach them all. That is, again, the case if the athlete has turned to the point of external validation and motivation. A world-class athlete who perseveres internal motivation and aspiration tends to trust their gut feelings more than the noise of society. These athletes, though, are often seen to continue being in sport in a different role or just not competing but still support the mastery and other artfulness of the sport.

After the Podium

Female athletes are used to being strong physically and mentally. Yet, after birth, the definition of strength changes drastically, and the majority of female athletes are not ready for it. Being one of the representatives of this demographic, I can attest that slowing down and going to smaller is bigger, less is more was a real challenge.

Originally, I was researching the subject of female bodily changes after professional sports and after pregnancy with a cesarian birth, as I was in constant pain. No doctors, therapists, scientists, holistic doctors, CT scans etc., were able to determine what was wrong until I dug into the micro muscles of the female body. The diaphragms of our bodies and how there are a billion muscles we don't see play a crucial role in the endocrine system, postpartum depression, and overall hormonal balance, which essentially affects the aging rate, regenerative capabilities of the body and mental clarity.

I must also state that I have not seen these muscles being trained in any female athletes. 100% of female athletes who started the training program had to be educated on the location of the muscles, sensations, and adjustments in movement.

One of the most difficult parts was to let go of measurements in the traditional sense of numbers and scales. The reliance fell solely on sensations. There are the muscles you don't see or touch but can only feel. 100% of participants referred to their body before as being "numb," as for the first 7-10 days, these female athletes were not able to "feel those muscles." Just because we don't see something doesn't mean it doesn't exist. Micro muscles don't get sore. Its movement is barely noticeable, and if you do more, you screw up.

You have to do less, gentler, slower. Something we athletes are rarely taught. Who would've thought that the position of our tongue affects our knees, feet, and pelvis?

During the first few years of motherhood, mothers are very psychologically and physiologically vulnerable. Lack of sleep, nutrition, societal pressures, and other external and internal factors affect the woman's nervous system.

Suppose the female athlete hasn't fully gone through the transition after sports. In that case, it can potentially wear out the nervous system to the extent of a nervous breakdown, depression, and suicidal condition, directly impacting the child/children. If the female athlete goes through pregnancy and shortly after is exposed to a high-pressure work environment where survival instinct is triggered, it can result in neurotic behaviour and in need for medication. The problem with the medication is that while it can certainly help and offset harmful behaviour, it doesn't address the cause, which is the overworked nervous system. Pair it with social media platforms and a never-ending stream of calls and emails from work; it is bound for disaster.

During the first few years of motherhood, what could help retired female mothers is prescribed rest to the point where it is an instruction and a rule. The reason for that is that these athletes often feel guilty about asking for a break, performing less than expected and generally not understanding that by becoming a mother, they took on a huge role, which naturally will take away from other areas of their lives before the baby was born.

I personally found that alcohol makes things even worse. What seems like relaxation is actually taping into the body's reserves. As I measured my sleep, hydration, heart rate, HRV and other components of my well-being, I saw the direct detrimental impact of alcohol, especially sleep, which is crucial for the restorative capabilities of the body.

It is even more important for new mothers who are constantly sleep-deprived. After observing myself and later other female athletes after giving birth, sleep seemed to be the number one solution to many struggles. Even short naps of 30 minutes during the day greatly affected mental clarity and irritability levels. Mind you, though, that those, who couldn't fall asleep, just lying down in a dark room with their eyes closed and no distraction in terms of visual or sound, even if it was relaxing music, still provided great benefits.

I found that coffee doesn't really provide energy. It dulls the sense of fatigue and tricks the body into thinking it doesn't need any rest.

After getting rid of the stimulants like coffee, sugars, early morning workouts etc., that tap into the body's reserves and age tremendously, it took a while to restore the balance between active stages of the day and slower ones.

I added more healthy fats like olive oil, fish oil and butter to my daily intake without affecting my weight or muscle mass. After nourishing my nervous system with fats, water, and sleep, I felt a big difference in my energy levels within the first month.

Another big component of female athlete anxiety levels was oral contraceptives and restoring the biological clock of their menstruation. One of the biggest challenges was giving up control, where it was no longer the external schedule driving decisions, plans and intentions but biological predisposition. Female athletes, who were used to pushing through, and neglecting their bodies' needs, often felt guilty about slowing down, measuring themselves against colleagues, where male professionals formed the majority.

These athletes were also shy to talk about their menstrual clock with their partners and spouses. Finding it an awkward topic, they would avoid drawing attention to it. They would see menstruation as a disadvantage of being a woman rather than a capacity of the body to grow life within itself.

In other words, speaking metaphorically, retired female athletes who gave birth are going through a double transition. When they lose their athletic identity, they also lose their teenage self and become a mature woman. Some resist both vigorously and try to remain a gritty girl athlete with the rebellious character of a teenager while fighting for the rights of the neglected and denying their female essence and biological difference from that of a male body.

These athletes would often embark on joining protests, "change the world," "break the system," etc. In our mutual findings, this is an attempt to resist natural progression, disagreement with the way things worked out in the past and an attempt to change the past by projecting it into the present.

Once the athlete was able to process and digest past situations and agree with natural life cycles, they were able to feel more wholesome, relaxed, and grounded. Their pace naturally slowed down, and they were no longer feeling like they were being chased or they needed to chase after plans, goals, dreams etc.

Chapter 14

Interpersonal Network

As pack animals, we humans need our network and social circle to thrive. As a pack, we survived for thousands of years. Being alone means death, so we fear being excluded from society/group. It's our self-preservation mechanism to stay together.

When we're active athletes, no matter how much we've achieved at that stage, we belong to professional sports. We identify with it and feel part of it. One understands the culture and the mindset, we feel at home. We know the ways. We can navigate the waters. Our belonging gives us an identity. We feel part of something bigger, something more powerful, with the same mentality, traditions, and values as us. We are family. We relate to one another.

Athletes lose their families, pack, and base when they leave sports. They are no longer living in the same rhythm as their family did. They don't eat the same way. They don't function the same. And no matter how good or strong their relationships were in this sports family; they lost those connections gradually until they became estranged. They no longer have the same topics to discuss or the same goals to achieve. Suddenly they become different.

After the Podium

They would have been with their sports family for two decades. They were figuring each other out, learning to function well, learning a specific communication style, to find themselves on their own to survive suddenly. Having to learn new skills, hard skills, and communication skills. It suddenly feels that their knowledge, skills, and physical abilities have no value to the new pack, the world they are trying to fit into. Unexpectedly their self-worth is shattered because almost everything they thought of as value inflated overnight.

It doesn't matter how far or how fast they can run, how deep they can dive, or how high they can jump. They didn't just lose their family. They lost themselves with it. Athletes will leave a part of themselves behind in professional sports, which is missing now. They don't feel whole anymore. When they miss, they reminisce and will lose themselves in the past period. They try to fill the void by setting new goals and embarking on new journeys, yet nothing feels the same.

Sadly, so many athletes turned to alcohol and drugs or even suicide. Crippling anxiety sometimes takes the best of us. The grief accompanying the loss of family, a sturdy comprehensive place in the sports society, is often unrecognized and undiagnosed because athletes are way too good at keeping a poker face or a happy mask for the outer world and themselves. "I am fine" is what athletes tell themselves as well as others. And courage is needed to admit the low point. But also let sadness and pain flood the void. Feel it, live through it, scar with it and eventually move on. Needless to say, that loneliness after sports is a very prominent feeling. Not because we don't have family or friends but because we don't have someone who understands our feelings. Even if they try, they won't be able to unless they go through it themselves.

That's why Athlete's Residence was born. This stage is very close to mourning a loss of a loved one, and yet it is different for athletes because we are a different breed. That's why some athletes stay in sports way past the average sports retirement age because the thought of becoming an exile is unbearable.

Interestingly, even within the sports world, athletes grieve differently based on the sports structure they came from.

If it was a team sport, they would grieve the loss of camaraderie, the brotherhood or sisterhood, that they were stronger together. When the team member retires, they no longer feel the entire spirit, no longer feel as solid or empowered. Sometimes the athlete would start looking for another team to replace a missing object of their identity. They might even be successful in finding a replacement for a while. Since they didn't go through the process of separation and grief, they will most likely continue going through situations where they will need to experience similar instances of leaving a team, a company, or even a family. They will share it over and over until they find the courage to process the grief and move on. As Freud said, what hasn't been processed is bound to repeat.

The longer the athlete pushes the process away, the more tired they will become physically and mentally. This is when we often witness low energy in seemingly healthy former athletes. They might eat healthily and exercise regularly. Yet can only make it through the day with supplements, coffee, energy drink or other nutritional supplements that boost energy. In the worst-case scenario, they turn to drugs, which squeeze their last little drop out for productivity.

Fear that this separation will eventually happen will wear a person down. They can't relax, and this will affect their sleep, more precisely, their deep sleep, which is responsible for the reparative quality of the brain and nervous system.

The athlete might even get 10 hours of sleep and feel more tired than before they went to sleep. The reason is that the psyche constantly needs to be alert and on guard because the potential threat might attack at any point. Keep the doors closed.

Constantly being afraid is a latent anxiety in the background. When this fear is unidentified, it can drive the person insane, deplete the nervous system, and even cause neurosis.

We can fix the sleep problem with supplements etc. Ultimately, we're treating the symptom and not the root cause. The root cause is the resistance to grieving and experiencing the emotional pain of losing a sports family. If the athlete felt that there is a home, a safe ground, where they can share their pain and not be alone in that process, it would enable them to have enough inner power to go through it rather than constantly try to avoid the inevitable and be on the run.

This might expose them to potentially experiencing prosecutor depression which Melanie Klein extensively describes in her works. This stems from athletes losing their social circle and their sports families. Back then, villages and tribes would get together to share a person's grief. They would support the person by lending them their emotional space, as they understood that the person in pain would start affecting the rest of the tribe. Hence, it was in their best interest to conquer the pain together. Together they could lift more than if the person was alone and solely put the entire weight on their shoulders.

Everyone joined in to preserve their healthy climate in the pack because they had a common goal of surviving and maintaining a healthy environment within the family of that tribe.

A different shade of losing sports family is observed in athletes of individual sports.

Such athletes tend to grow up in a sports environment. They know that if they stand out in their performance, they get a team of people to support them in their pursuit of high performance.

Here, the athlete was a manageable part of the team rather than a moving force, the primary tool. Where what's expected of them is to give 100% of their effort to reach the highest results, having a support team behind them all wanting to succeed.

Everyone is invested in that athlete's success. Since that success equals their success. Athletes, even though working on a mutual goal together with the team, have their primary focus on themselves. These athletes are trained in a very narrow tunnel vision. They rely on the team to complete tasks they are responsible for, so the athlete can focus 100% of their attention on their performance.

When individual sports athletes retire from sports, they often feel very self-sufficient. They believe that if they work hard enough, everything else will fall into place. They know, they are not lazy. They know they can work hard and are used to having a team behind them that wants them to succeed.

When athlete tries to build a business, they go all in. They work day and night. They hustle, make sacrifices, and fail the company.

100% of athletes I interviewed who tried starting a business right after a sports career couldn't make it profitable.

100% of these athletes agreed that they tried doing it all themselves and could not build a team with integrity within a mutual goal and synchronized efforts.

Athletes agreed that they think of themselves as leaders, willing to take risks and responsibilities, and dedicated to their teams and business. Yet, their biggest disappointment was the need for the right people to join their team. Athletes' communication skills, expectations and work ethics are often different from people who have never worked in a sports environment. Some called it a cultural shock. They thought of the rest of the world the same way as they saw the sports world. Where athletes' dedicated teams are reliable, and everyone is synchronized in reaching their mutual goal. The awakening was a rough period that discouraged many from finding their "dream team."

Building an efficiently working team is a skill often attached to a leader's symbol. Yet not every leader is a team builder. Only some team builders are or want to be a leader. The challenge in the modern day with building a sturdier reliable team is a need for more trust in people in general.

People are in survival mode, where everything becomes personal versus communal. Where people are looking after themselves rather than the team. Trust is built over time. Going through the best and the worst. That's why athletes have so much confidence in their team in sports because they went through multiple ups and downs together.

They know the character of their pack. It doesn't mean that there is no conflict. They can work through disagreements and work together efficiently in a healthy environment.

When athletes build a team for their business, they look at brand-new relationships. Relationships that haven't had a test of time and adversity.

The communication skills and conflict resolution they've learned over decades in sports no longer apply because people outside sports are different. No wonder athletes feel disoriented. Everything they know and can doesn't work in this new world.

Part II

Chapter 15

The Pack

We used to function as a pack. Some tribes today, who stayed off the grid, continue to operate in packs, aka tribes.

What is a pack?

It is a well-organized group, in our case, humans, who utilize their best talents and abilities to serve a bigger purpose of the group (survival and comfortable quality of life) rather than individual agendas. It is a system, a mechanism, where everyone belongs to their place with assigned responsibilities and duties based on their abilities. A whole is bigger than the sum of parts. A pack forms a whole "system" that is self-sufficient, self-organizing and self-governed.

Back in the days, when belonging to a pack was vital for a person to survive, self-identity was barely a problem. From an early age, a child exhibits traits the pack could utilize.

After the Podium

Let's discuss the simplified arrangement of the pack.

About 80% are workers with physical abilities, stamina, and vital health to do "the work," not to "think."

Others did the thinking. While people work, they need guards to protect the pack from predators or neighbouring tribes. People with excellent eyesight, attention to detail and a generally somewhat anxious temperament would stay on guard during the day. During the night, however, day guards would need to be replaced by night guards, who have intense hearing and can stay up at night and find comfort in being alone and quiet.

While workers were working and guards guarding, the pack needed hunters to hunt. Hunters would run fast, track the prey, and have sensitive skin sensitive pain, which would drive hunters to create traps and weapons, to minimize the possibility of being cut and scratched. Hunters would be the efficient ones.

Then we have people who are naturally curious about everything, new food, new land, new ways of building things etc. They would try things out and then come back to the tribe and report, what was working, what was not, which berry was poisonous, which one was not etc.

These guys wouldn't stay around much, as they always lived their life as an adventure, so someone had to capture all the information to teach. So, we have teachers in the pack "who know," who will then teach everyone else, starting with kids, about everything the pack was able to learn over the years.

Then, of course, we need a leader to expand and develop the tribe. The chief. One that is self-devoted to the pack and gains pleasure in seeing his tribe being taken care of. His advisor, the shaman, would possess the traits of acquiring a different knowledge through his intuition, connection with nature and other senses that are not perceived by the eye. The shaman would also be a healer who intuitively knows the herbs that treat a specific condition. It was an animal-like instinct. While the leader would be the "face" of the pack, the shaman would usually stay in the shadow, in the background. He would only want to interact with the crowd directly if very necessary.

As you can see, the roles in the pack or a tribe were assigned based on genetic predisposition.

You wouldn't argue that a person with poor eyesight would be a lousy day guard and would put the entire pack in danger by missing rivalling tribe hiding in the bush. So, the pack, wanting to survive, would put a person with the best eyesight to heighten the chances of survival. The same goes for someone with intuition and the ability to "read the room" being put to work building homes when he can barely lift a small rock.

After the Podium

Even though homo-sapiens were relatively primitive at first, the need to survive called for the most efficient organization, something today in the era of high-tech and replacement of human labour became very problematic, partially because our "tribes" became too large. Our current lifestyle in big cities has become quite isolated, where the need for connections and relationships is replaced with money.

If before, I would have to make an effort to get to know my neighbours, make a connection, accept their flaws etc., so later I could ask to babysit my child, watch my house while I'm away etc. Today I can hire a "nanny," buy a home alarm etc.

I can argue that primitive tribes thousands of years ago had higher emotional intelligence than many do today. Sure, they weren't able to "build businesses." Still, they could build connections, adapt to other people's personalities, and organize themselves efficiently where their talent was of use. In contrast, others had a place to use their strongest abilities without the need to be universal and, as a result, not applicable anywhere because no talent would stand out and rather be mediocre than outstanding, yielding the best outcomes of applied attention to one specific task.

Today, an average job post would have "multitasking" as a required skill. In other words, "We need three people to do a great job for what we need. Instead, we will hire one person who will perform average and be confused about who they actually are and what they do to make a positive change".

The more blurred an employee's responsibilities, the lower the results. The less defined the field of expertise, the longer it will take for the company to grow and succeed.

But genes obviously work not only in business and work, which is almost the basis of our identification since we all want to do what we are meant to do when we are born. This is why we see a massive influx of people seeking life's purpose. They are looking for a place where they belong, where what they do matters.

Being universal creates problems and stagnation in every part of our lives, be it family, community, work etc. Because being universal takes away "our place," a place in the society we were given when we were born. If I was born with an endless interest in exploring new things and am excited to tell everyone about it, there's a place for me in the pack I was born into. Nature, you know, is self-regulating. (Please watch "The biggest little Farm" again). If I was born into that pack, there's a place for me to take, by definition.

I am needed, and my talents are appreciated. Now with universalism, I can't occupy a place fully. I don't fit into that place because it's built for one specific talent. The place is in a star shape, but I, being universal, possess round sides, square sides and maybe even a zigzag side. I won't fully fit in and will feel I need to be more because I'm no longer a full star. I'm universal. I could've been a star from the get-go and, by now, would've developed some extraordinary traits.

Lots of parents and society, in general, have this thing where they think they know what's best for their child when it comes to their talent development. Of course, because our schools grade everyone against a standard and an average, kids who come out of school aim to be average because if they are "circles" who didn't succeed at learning to be a "square," won't graduate from high school, because "being square" is a requirement for graduation.

So kids are being tortured into becoming average and then face the dilemma of not feeling like they belong in society.

Not everyone is born a leader; they don't have to be one. They need to master their talents. You would hardly find a parent who doesn't want their child to be a leader. "Leader" became the new "Jesus" of our society. We have a very distorted vision of who a leader is.

We see endless lineups of people who want to become "triangles," even though they are "circles" and could be perfect "circles" if they looked for their place and not for the "best" position, according to society or parents.

If simplified, we have eight simple genes and eight simple roles in the pack. The genes evolved throughout the life of humans. The genes are responsible for survival. Some gene lines survived, and some didn't.

By genes I mean of course metaphorical genes, not the genes you find in a lab. Genes are a program that the body learned over thousands of years about how to interact with the environment.

A lot of people think that the fittest means the strongest. No, the fittest means to fit into your designed place perfectly and develop your survival talent to its best potential.

Essentially, the genes are there for when danger comes, and our body unconsciously knows how to survive. The stem cell will always prevail over the logical brain.

The hunter will run away fast, without thinking about what he should do, because there's no time for thinking and analyzing. He'll be eaten by then.

It is an automatic response of our immune system, of our survival mechanism, developed through thousands of years of survival. Our stem cell information is "embedded" into our bodily system, our DNA. Before the brain can think, the body has already acted. Be it sweat, clenched jaw, watering eyes, numb limbs or any other "action" the brain can't control or wasn't fast enough to manage.

After the Podium

Whether or not we want it to react a certain way to stress is irrelevant. The body, the gene, will do what proved to be the recipe for survival. Period.

I don't support the saying "nature vs nurture." I keep nurturing nature for maximum beneficial results. Nature vs nurture, to me, is like being born a bunny and nurtured to become a lion. Very doubtful approach if you ask me.

So, the fastest and easiest way of finding one's place, feeling fulfilled and knowing that what we do matters is to discontinue the pursuit of universal. Drop the belief that we can be anything and everything. Go back to the "default settings" of what we were born as, strip off the knowledge of what we should be, and start nurturing the genes that give us an advantage vs averaging us out.

That's when we gain the certainty of the future, the sturdiness of the ground underneath us, the precise direction of our journey and the bliss of fulfilling interpersonal connections that complement each other for more extraordinary achievements.

Valeria Tsoy

Chapter 16

Nature vs Nurture

I want to present another component that many people disregard. It is our nature.

What are we born with when we show up in this world? What does our DNA transmute and radiate into this world? What happens when we fight our nature, and how can we scale back to the basics to get to know who we are in the world we were born to be doing?

About 6000 years ago, we became Homo sapiens. We soon understood that surviving in the Pack is more manageable than living alone. We formed packs. We needed to determine our social roles as we quickly figured out that if the entire Pack goes hunting and little offspring are left behind alone, they get killed either by a sable-tooth tiger; (I know, these didn't exist, but it makes it a good character for the story), or by a neighbouring pack, who were fighting for the territory.

So, we needed guards who'd protect the Pack. These guards would look very closely into the prairies, memorizing every piece of grass, every rock, and every stick, and if something would be out of order, quickly notified the Pack about the danger. Of course, there was a learning curve; sometimes, they would miss the danger and get eaten. Throughout generations, a visual gene has developed. They are always anxious and scared ones, keeping their eyes open as wide as possible and afraid to turn their backs into the open space. People with this gene are natural-born worriers.

They worry. That's their nature. They fear that someone or something will attack them from behind when they don't SEE.

These people always choose a place in the restaurant to lean back onto a wall and scan the environment for potential danger. They don't like being in a crowd. They stay on the side so that they can see everyone and everything. They are very attentive to details, and 80% of information receive from the visual channel.

They worry a lot because their imagination is mighty, and they can imagine things that could only happen in their imagination and hardly in reality. Their fantasy world is the richest of all other genes. The ancient fear of being eaten alive prevails over logic because their body knows. The body needs to live and survive.

What do you think would act faster in dangerous or stressful situations? Logical thinking or the body's intellect, the stem cell, that has been surviving for thousands of years perfecting the skill and carrying information of the best practices? You guessed it, the stem cell always wins. 100%.

Valeria Tsoy

We determine the gene by the unconscious behaviour of the body. The body language or automatic physiological response of the body.

When the visual gene is afraid and nervous, it smells like fear. These people don't need to tell us anything. They smell, so we feel nervous and uncomfortable next to them when they are scared because that's their purpose. Their body stinks of fear, so everyone in the Pack can run away and hide while the predator devours the body of the visual gene.

However, during a time of peace, this gene notices all the delicate world around us. Their spectrum of colour recognition is the widest one of all. And so, when they are off their guarding shift, they can relax and put the colour recognition skill to work. They were the ones who started creating paint and paintings, decorating the cave, and putting flowers in the hair.

At least our bodies follow a natural cycle of work and rest. So, when the visual gene rested, who was stepping in to fill in?

Are we capable of staying awake 24 hours a day? Of course not. The visual gene kept the day shifts, but the following gifted gene stepped in when the nighttime came. We rely on our hearing when our eyes can't see.

Here comes the acoustic gene. People who hear the stick break under the paws of a leopard at night. Those who hear the sounds that the wind brings. Who spend the majority of their time in the silence of the night. People who tend to listen more than they speak. Of course, they had to be quiet at night not to attract the predators' attention. They are the ones who can hear the language of nature, space, and the stars. They look at night at the stars and wonder. Their thinking happens when the sounds are dimmed.

They understand and hear things differently. When we speak, they don't listen to what we say, but how we say it, how our voice sounds, and what vibration the air creates. These people usually speak multiple languages because they can absorb and hear the language and its pronunciation rather than logically try to remember and store it in their heads. These people at business meetings can determine whether the deal is right not by the numbers and graphs presented on the screen but by how the presenter sounded.

These people often say, "Sounds good, or something doesn't sound right here." Many people think it is intuition, but it is a language that only acoustic genes can hear and understand.

They are often introverts who prefer to work in a quiet environment, better even alone. They don't like loud music or big gatherings. Inspiration comes at night when everything is quiet, and they can hear. The space, the wind of changes, themselves. Of course, they are often seen creating music and languages, like computer coding. They love mystical things. They're usually innovators who get their ideas out of thin air.

Conversely, this gene can become melancholic and depressed if left unattended. They think that they are going crazy because suddenly they hear these voices in their head, and they don't know what to do with them. Back in the day, the acoustic guard would've come to the chief and told him that the ancestor ghosts said a pack nearby was planning an attack on their tribe, and they needed to be prepared. So, the chief would gather warriors expecting an attack, and it would save their lives.

Today if a person says, "I can feel/hear something is coming our way," people would offer this person psychological help. But all they need to do is materialize the information that came to them in text, painting, clothing, or anything else that people without acoustic genes can understand and relate to on a material plane.

The intellect of an acoustic gene is beyond this world because it comes from elsewhere. These are generally scientists that develop spaceships. Coders of new technology. Poets and writers can put information into words and between the lines where the readers will find additional meaning to the text and won't be able to explain what moved their souls.

While the guards were guarding, the hunters were hunting.

The skin gene is entering the stage.

After the Podium

They were the first to realize that tomorrow would come, and the mammoth didn't need to be eaten entirely today. It can be stored for tomorrow, so there will be no need to hunt for tomorrow. Efficiency is their slogan. Maximum impact with minimum effort. These people live to save—time, effort, energy, food, scraps and, of course, money. The skin is what shapes up the body essentially. It restricts the form. So, the skin gene is the one that restricts themselves and others. Limitation. They are generally slim and fit by nature. They organize and put order and rules in place.

They were the ones who thought of a bridge across the river when the Pack needed to travel onto the other side of the riverbank instead of walking for a day to the spot where the current wasn't strong to get to the other side and hunt. Walk back the same way to bring back the game. Skin Gene decided to save time and effort, so they thought of a log across the river. Instead of running after the mammoth, they considered digging up a hole as a trap.

Their energy supply is explosive but limited. They can run fast, but not far. They can work and think fast, but not long and steadily paced.

They are the ultimate problem solvers. And sometimes can even fall prey to their own gift by creating problems, so they can solve them. It's like a never-ending entertaining game for them. If they are not given a proper position in society where their problem-solving gift is utilized, they can become anxious, as the need to contribute is not fulfilled. One of their biggest mistakes is that they must devise a problem solution and execute it too. Well, not really, but more about it later.

The skin gene is there to better and optimize the Pack's life. On the flip side, when stressed, they become greedy and want to collect everything, especially when it's free. Like in the anecdote, they're also the ones who would eat a bucket of rotten apples. A man had a bucket of apples. One apple started to rot. So, the man decided to eat that one first and keep the other ones nice and fresh. The next day he noticed another apple started to rot. He ate that one and kept the other ones fresh. And so forth, until he ate a bucket of rotten apples.

A fulfilled skin gene will help you figure out how to cheaper build a boat. Would come to the tribe and teach everyone how to make better boats faster and more affordable. On the flip side, when the skin gene is stressed and doesn't understand its role in society, it would keep his new finding a secret. Build those boats himself and then sell them for more to the Pack, so he is the only one who benefits financially from his discovery. A stressed skin gene takes and doesn't give/serve.

When the skin gene is "sick," it cares about how to become richer. To be better than the neighbour. They become unhealthy and competitive instead of adapting their gene to the circumstances and finding a way to serve the whole in the best possible way, so everyone in the Pack can benefit from their existence.

After the Podium

Because every gene was developed so Homo sapiens could survive, each plays its distinct role in the Pack.

The Pack smells when the gene is sick and starts distrusting such people. An unhealthy skin gene often has very few friends—mostly business partnerships where they feed off each other. A healthy gene, however, can develop a close circle of friends; generally, this close circle acts like a pack.

If the skin gene understands that her talents are for everyone to benefit from, then this gene gets the support of the Pack and its trust and inclusiveness. The skin gene is in its best development as part of the Pack. Its worst presentation is a lone wolf with beneficial connections who also doesn't care about them but is using them as a link, just as they are using the others. Naturally, an underdeveloped skin gene will prioritize material wealth and possessions over relationships. They would think their material wealth determines their self-worth, so they often upgrade life partners the wealthier they get.

Developed skin gene is a brilliant salesperson and is business savvy. It is very vibrant and energizing to be around. They're quick and agile. They are primary managers though not workers. And that's where their problem-solving skill comes in. They manage a group of people to execute the solution.

While hunters were away, someone needed to teach the young flock survival skill. The anal gene comes to the fore. It's called this way because when this gene gets stressed, the sphincters in the anus tighten up first and foremost. That's their unconscious stress response. They can get constipation and nausea in response to frustration.

Anal Gene is a true master of their art. Whichever industry it is, they are meticulous about their craft and performance. They are perfectionists who ensure the task is performed to the best possible standard. They love their standards and manuals. They are by the book and expect everyone else to be like that too. They are slow and square. Their seat needs to be comfortable because they spend a lot of time sitting. They perform slowly and methodically, dotting all the I's and crossing all the t's. They get very frustrated if they get rushed.

Anal gene is very family oriented. The most important value for them is praise, recognition, and respect. They prefer a recognition diploma at work rather than a pay raise without public acknowledgment. They rarely move careers, houses, or counties. They stay put.

The anal gene is entirely predictable. They do as the book says. They do as they were taught, and they hate anything new or any change and have difficulty adjusting to the faster pace.

They love to teach. Better yet, they love "to know" and give advice based on what they read or were taught.

After the Podium

A Frustrated anal gene will try to undervalue and cover in dirt things they find around them. They start looking for flaws in anything they see, touch, or interact with. They would also start looking to improve others and treat them as a pet project they would like to bring to perfection. Because they are slow at processing new things, they crave "stability," meaning no change, even if it's a change in the room furnishings. They want things their way. They crave control so that nothing causes them discomfort.

They get used to things, and it's hard to let go. They are people of the past. They remember things that happened 40-50 years ago, like yesterday. They often have nostalgia. The way things were in the past is always perceived better than in the present. When stressed, they usually want to go back to the way things once were. They reminisce and never quite get over their past experiences and let go.

The anal gene makes things last. To last for centuries. They build sturdy homes for generations after them. They carry out traditions the family had for a thousand years. Slowly but surely. They plan and hate the unknown, unpredictable, and unmeasurable. They stick to the plan no matter what. They are a tank. And if an obstacle impairs their plans, they try to bulldoze through it. A determined direction sometimes prevails over the common sense of getting around rather than through. They can get very stubborn if frustrated.

If we only relied on how anal gene lives, we would hardly acquire any new knowledge or discover anything outside the known.

Valeria Tsoy

So, the oral gene is the one the anal gene can't stand, but oh so much depends on.

The oral gene that likes to try everything new. New food, new experiences, new clothes. Anything. It is the most curious gene of all. Oral genes barely remember the past because if they did, they would be afraid to attempt that thing again.

The anal gene calls the oral gene "stupid" because the oral gene doesn't retain the "knowledge" of a "failure" experience. If it did, it would fill up at some point and get too satisfied and comfortable to keep exploring, and we couldn't learn from their experiences, mistakes, and accomplishments.

So anal gene needs to sometimes follow the oral gene to "record" information, while the oral has already moved on to the next "new thing" and forgotten what he was talking about. The good thing is the anal was able to catch it fast enough in their notes.

Oral (mouth) is how this gene interacts with the world. They consume orally, but they give orally too. They experience and then tell. Experience and then tell. Nothing will stop the oral gene from telling you about their experience if they have not let it all out yet. Their archetypal role in the Pack was to yell so loudly that the tiger was approaching so everyone would hear them and have time to run away, hide or get their weapons. They are loud.

But they would also be the ones who would try anything on the food menu. Sometimes they would die by eating the poisonous berry, but that way, saving a pack of a hundred. Sometimes they would try to jump off things and hurt themselves. Every experience, big or small, has a paramount and worthy outcome. Without it, we wouldn't be able to evolve. The oral gene tries. Everything. They try, so others don't. They heal faster than others. So, they can continue experimenting.

Suppose the anal gene wants a predictable outcome and writes a manual for a repeated, identical result. In that case, the oral gene is a scientist who experiments and doesn't get bogged down by any result. Anal gene would call it a mistake. Oral will call it an experience, result or information, an outcome. They live for an outcome.

If an oral gene starts treating "unsatisfactory results" as mistakes, it will kill it. They would stop experimenting and performing everyday science. Its curiosity will diminish, and it will get sick. An oral gene can't have a goal to achieve. It needs freedom of whatever outcome because it feeds off the unknown. What happens if I do this start-up? What happens if I mix up these ingredients?

A goal, on the other hand, is a known endpoint that kills the fun. This restriction prevents the oral gene from exercising its full potential and natural instinct to explore.

Valeria Tsoy

The urethral gene gives it all away when the skin gene tries to collect as much as possible. The urethral gene is thought to be the chief, the leader, who gives away the riches to the Pack, so it flourishes. The urethral gene starts having kidney problems and urethral tract infection, as it restricts urine from coming out or being unable to hold. This gene sees a bigger picture. It tells a few steps ahead. This gene is a strategist and a leader. Its main concern is the survival of the Pack. If sacrifices must be made to win a battle, the urethral gene will not hesitate. It doesn't have attachments to individual faiths if it puts the survival of the entire Pack at risk. So, in business, a urethral gene will not hesitate to fire his closest professional connections if their performance or underperformance jeopardizes the company's livelihood.

She doesn't measure situations and choices by right and wrong. She does what's necessary and is not afraid to be the "bad guy" in the eyes of the masses because she understands that what she sees in the long run, the masses can't. The masses see what's under their nose. The urethral gene sees generational impacts. Her plans are long-term, and her dedication to those plans is not wavered by small stuff on the way.

It is also one of the most potent and fertile genes. If half of the Pack was killed in an attack, this gene ensures impregnation or gives birth to as many human species as possible.

After the Podium

The urethral gene takes pleasure in giving and is just. The point is not to give away riches to anyone and everyone. The point is to give to those who need it.

The anal gene would give each family an equal amount of grain. It is fair. The urethral gene will provide to a family of three 6 pounds of grain and a family of five 10 pounds. That is just. When war would come, anal would have a standard for every family of 2 men going to war. The urethral will call every man in the family to go.

If the urethral gene went hunting with the Pack, it would be the one to have the right to feed first and ensure that everyone will be fed in proper and necessary amounts.

Then we have the chief's advisor. A gene that "smells danger." The smell gene does not have the same sense of smell as the oral gene, whether it smells tasty or not. The smell gene smells when something fishy is going on. It distrusts the words people say. It trusts only its instincts. This gene is the library of survival of the human species. Everything our DNA collected thus far is contained as information in this gene in the form of an instinct encoded into our cells. It's a stem cell.

The advisor is the master of deciphering intrigues and conspiracies but is also the one who creates those. This gene usually doesn't like being around people for a long time, as it gets overstimulated by the "smells" of people. Each person has a distinct smell. This smell is information that we consciously rarely recognize and decode. Yet the smell gene can do so if it's in tune with its instincts. This gene is the survivor. Its biological role is to survive and carry on the information it contains. Smell Gene will unconsciously miss a bus that got into an accident and killed all the passengers; will trip over a branch, fall, and avoid a bullet that someone shot in a mass shooting.

It lives. No matter what. It lives to carry on the information.

The smell gene would show up in the company at the most critical time and find the best way out. They are excellent crisis managers as long as they trust their instincts and do not know logic. The logical path led the company into the mess it found itself in. The smell gene is "sent" to the company so the system will survive. If the smell gene has left for no obvious reason, chances are the system is doomed to collapse.

The smell gene wants to stay in the shadows. It likes something other than publicity. It whispers into the ear of the urethral gene and lets them deliver the news and be the face of power. While the urethral gene is a charismatic leader, the smell gene is the vizier, whom everyone fears and would rather be on its better list than not. The Pack is cautious when the smell gene starts "smelling around." They get this unease, this shiver up the spine, because nothing can be hidden from the smell gene, no matter how much you try to mask it, be it perfume, flowers or any other scent.

After the Podium

Then the Pack needs muscles. Muscles that work and don't ask questions. Drum rolls, please... the last gene of the Marvelous 8, the muscle gene.

The muscle gene is one of the simplest genes, yet one of the most vital. The one that people need for heavy lifting and the actual physical work. In the modern world, if a person has a muscle gene, it is paramount that they engage in physical activity, heavy lifting and sweat. Muscle gene starts dying the fastest if it isn't stimulated either in the gym or in any other heavy lifting in the garden, farm, loading boxes and moving furniture. It is doubtful that muscle genes will find themselves in an office environment.

The simpler the job, the better. They can lift, push, do the hard work, come home, open a can of beer at the end of the day and watch their sports channel. This is what makes them happy. They don't care about going to a 5-star resort in the Bahamas. They feel fulfilled by a simple life, simple job, and simple show. They don't question themselves with the purpose of life. They are happy, and nothing bothers them. And that is their natural role. This is who they are meant to be and what they are intended to do. So please, let go of the muscle gene. Don't call them uneducated, stupid or any of that. They are perfect in the way they are. And we all benefit from them being simple and unambitious. We need them.

Everyone is born with a purpose and a perfect ratio to what the world needs most. I am returning to the "Biggest Little Farm" movie.

Valeria Tsoy

Everything we see in the society of animals works precisely like that in the community of humans. It's a self-organizing system with its intellect, which is far smarter than the individual intellects of humans. And if we think that we know what the world, nature etc., needs, we think too highly of ourselves.

Now that we discussed our genes, it is clearer that we function best as a pack. Our gifts and talents are brought to their highest potential in the Pack. We are all interconnected. Somebody's gift is only complimentary to our gifts. We're exploring our potential, whether it's our bodies, minds, brains, or creativity, to benefit the Pack and make our lives better, not just one person or family to benefit.

There's a perfect analogy about an Ant and three fingers.

Suppose we put down three fingers around an ant. In that case, its brain won't be able to comprehend that these three fingers are not just three separate columns, but the three fingers of one hand are part of a whole human. Oftentimes our minds need to comprehend how much influence we have and how many people we can affect.

Another excellent example of our influence on many moving pieces is a situation with traffic. Imagine you were driving and got distracted. You cause a collision with another car. It was rush hour, so immediately, cars started to slow down. It's very strange, but if you looked at the traffic from a plane flying over this highway, you would see how the traffic started moving backwards. Some call it a visual illusion. It is an inertia energy that was redirected back. Like a stream of water that hits a dam, like a wave that hits the wall and redirects the upcoming wall waves backwards.

One person can make the energy of traffic move backwards, but now hundreds, if not thousands, of people are affected. And in these hundreds of thousands, someone can give birth in a car. Have a heart attack, get frustrated, yell at their boss, and get fired. You can continue the list of scenarios that could happen. The possibilities are endless.

But the fact is that you might never even know that these people exist. You will never meet them and discover how their story unravelled because of the traffic jam you caused. But the fact of the matter of your impact stays the same. So next time we think our actions are insignificant, think about the traffic jam again. What we do matters. It does affect people around us. Our genes matter because nature has this weird but precise way of balancing itself; we just need to let it organize itself by organizing us.

Our genes matter. They are needed. When we try to be or become somebody else, even if the person is admirable and noble, we still do ourselves, and others disfavour. Because a lion will always be given a gazelle to eat even though giraffes look very healthy, and the lions want to become vegan. And zebras will always be given grass no matter how hard they try to become a predator and hunt some mice.

Kidneys will always be given urine, and if it's given blood like the heart they want to be, blood will destroy the kidneys. It's one thing to have skills and talents. It's another to have them fulfilled by opportunities. But say a boy in Ethiopia is born with phenomenal violin-playing abilities. Still, unless he hears the violin, tries it, and learns to play, no one will ever know that another violin artist was born. How do your opportunities meet your talents and skills?

Well, first, it is the direction we're choosing. Is it for ourselves solely, or is it for our Pack? Michael Jordan was once asked why he gives it all every time he plays, even when the advantage over the other team is humongous. He replied that people come to watch him. They come for a show. There may be a kid whom Michael will inspire to take up basketball, and he would become the greatest player.

Remember, what we do matters; we are changing lives directly or indirectly for better or worse. A lot of athletes, when they perform, are looking to take. Attention, compliments, praise. To make the list of best-performing athletes to make money. In their head, every competition is not necessarily a way to give themselves to the spectator. There is a dollar sign next to performance ranking and ego pampering in their head.

After the Podium

It's a hard switch in thinking. Because athletes are trained to go after things, achieve goals, win, fight, defend the title, and take the title away. It's a battlefield where a fight or flight response is the primary one. We can hardly imagine how "survival" would think of giving or serving. On the flip side, we just spoke about internal motivation when something within ourselves is yearning to come out. When we feel this way, we either suppress it, or will it actualize and manifest? No greed is stopping us from giving. The river is overflowing and would provide plenty because there is No Fear that we won't have enough.

Each one of us is full of something, especially concerning our genes. An acoustic gene might be full of poems or music, and a visual may be full of paintings, movies, and theatre decorations. Envision! The urethral gene might be full of crazy futuristic ideas for a screenplay or new movie shooting methods. The gene of smell is full of the sense of direction to take the company to avoid the crisis. A muscle gene is so full of physical power that it may develop a whole field to plant crops. An anal gene might be so full of knowledge, and they can't help but teach and tell stories and myths.

A skin gene might be full of ideas for making an existing business more efficient, a car consuming less fuel, a plant needing less heat etc. Only when we are trying to defend or pretend, or our logical brain is driving us away from our natural talent, do we feel we have

Valeria Tsoy

to save a bit for and off ourselves? When we are in our natural environment, there is no deficit in what and how much we can give.

If I am a different species from my neighbour, knowing how to be me, I have no problem with who they are, but I also don't want to be the way they are. A zebra doesn't care to be a chipmunk.

Our brains are there to solve a problem. Being me, the way I was born is not a problem. My mom and dad are not 100% aligned with me. We carry all eight genes within us, just by how nature evolves, but some are dominant, and some are dormant. A dog, part of the canine family, won't be a fox. Better yet, it doesn't want/need to be a fox. Better to master the body of a dog than try to be or pretend to be a fox. The body knows what it is and won't back down, no matter what the brain thinks. The body is more intelligent than the brain.

When stepping away from our natural talent, it feels like we have to be economical about it or learn how to be a leader, entrepreneur, visionary, hardworking salesman, caretaker, etc.

So, let's say we have 60% of urethral gene and 30 acoustic, and the rest are two or three percent. In this case, we see a natural-born leader. The chief of the tribe. He writes music and unites people in his tribe with sound. Now he tries to sell his music and starts acting like a skin gene. He would immediately find it hard. So, he goes to a sales training. Graduates from Harvard Business School, only to find out that he spent half of his life trying to bring to the highest potential a gene he possesses only a percent or two, completely wasting the gift of which he already had 60% and 30% predominantly. It's like trying to complete a tower of 100 floors. You are given one structure where 60 floors are already completed. And another one where it is only the foundation done. Which one would you choose to continue to develop?

Same thing with genes. Ideally, the urethral gene would have continued to develop the combination of the urethra and acoustic gene and hired a skin gene to sell. Anal to ensure everything goes through correctly. Oral to tell everyone about this music. Muscle to work on setting up the stage. The gene of smell keeps an eye on how the crowd moves at the concert and how security needs to act accordingly.

You see, being everything for everyone is pointless. We're all interconnected and form a perfect Organism. And if we all do, what we were born for, we work smoothly, filling up gaps for each other. On the other hand, if a skin gene goes through leadership training, it will be a waste of time and money.

We can always take a big perspective and look at the world. And notice that we just recently went through a skin phase of development, which characterizes fast growth and efficiency. Before then, we saw the development of the anal phase, where things from architecture to machinery were built sturdy to last for ages.

The skin gene is war hungry. They are aggressive. Of course, and they used to be warriors. They are hunters. Every athlete has a skin gene in one proportion or the other. It might not be the predominant gene, but it is a fact that if an athlete achieves the status of a high-performance athlete, the skin gene is a gene that does influence them.

Knowing the gene composition helps predict the shadow and high potential behaviour. Shadow or just a different side of the coin of 1 gene will always come out when a person is under a high-stress period. Of course, the transition from sports is one of them. So, for example, skin genes will become hectic. They are already fast, but they might become extremely fussy or hasty. They would hustle to do millions of things at once. A stressed skin gene goes into problem-solving mode immediately. They are very sudden and become uncomfortably aggressive. Suppose they need to make a plan for sales.

In that case, they will become too aggressive in sales, and many people might become uncomfortable and angry with them and their approach. Skin gene doesn't like to contemplate. When they are stressed, they like to act/fight. They love going to war and showing who's the boss in the room. They are highly egocentric and can be blinded by blood thirst when making decisions.

For this skin gene, going for an intensive run before making big decisions is always beneficial. It clears their head and, on the cellular level, imitates the hunt back in the day. Biochemically it signals stem cells that the body is serving its purpose and can relax. I've seen some athletes would take it to the next level. They would compete against public transportation in the city. They would get double the enjoyment from fast running and also beating the bus.

Frequently entrepreneurs need to track why they started their businesses. They get too entertained and amused by the fight for dominance in the market. They would want to beat the competition and become focused on that rather than focusing on the customer and how to make their product or service better for them. Same with athletes. If the athlete is solely focused on beating the competition, and forgetting the spectators, who came to see the show, they would soon realize that they can only do their sport because of people who are interested in it.

A brilliant battlefield for the skin gene is the court. The Warriors absolutely love a good fight. Skin gene doesn't shy away from cheating into the win either.

Skin gene likes to fight. It is the most aggressive of all genes. Today social norms allow aggression to be expressed within the standards of our civilized society. Often times when we look back at humans, we see them as Barbarians without any morals or compassion. Of course, back in the day, aggression served as a vital part of survival. Kill or be killed.

Valeria Tsoy

Today aggression is still part of our lives, but somehow it is considered bad. And so, we try to hide, suppress, or camouflage it. Passive aggression is still aggression, just expressed differently, for example, through humour, excessive politeness, and even self-victimization and putting people on a guilt trip. Every athlete has aggression as part of them, and every human has aggression as part of them. It is a psychological energy given to us to withstand external and internal pressures.

And every athlete has a skin gene. What makes a difference is whether the gene is developed and can freely express itself or is suppressed and denied the right to come out.

The thing is that almost every person on earth would love to have a strong skin gene. Of course, it's also very beneficial in the era of the skin gene. However, when it comes to the other side of the coin, its weakness is when the survival mode is turned on. No one wants to come close to the skin gene, even those who possess it and can develop it to its highest potential. Naturally, every gene has its strengths and weaknesses.

Athletes with a significant portion of the skin gene under unimaginable pressure tend to push harder, fight, sacrifice, do more, and ramp up their speed until they collapse. The tension such behaviour creates in the psyche locks the thinking into a loop. At that point, it's not the logical or rational brain that's working. The stem cell takes charge.

After the Podium

In survival mode, the stem cell will always overpower, and the instincts will kick in. Compared to our logical brain, a stem cell has the advantage of thousands of years of survival memory. The goal of the body is to survive, whether it is moral or not, in any given situation. The logical brain only has a few decades of knowledge and development.

The mechanism, of course, served quite a few athletes during the competition. Ultramarathoners, for example, continued to run without sleep, rest and nourishment; some were even injured. When self-preservation instinct is turned off because it would enforce defence and firewall, it tells us to stop, rest and preserve ourselves when the brain becomes tired. When the body goes through a chemical reaction of life-threatening circumstances, it will employ a proven mechanism that it has used for thousands of years. It will either run, fight, or freeze. We can do nothing to change the memory of thousands of years that our genes inherited and implemented.

This is evolution. Each time the gene acted on instinct, it survived. Information got recorded in the cell and stored for the next generation. If another stem cell survival attack were to flee, which happened repeatedly, it would record that as the best-serving survival mechanism—the same thing with freeze. When Athletes get worked up, and the pressure is unbearable, they have reported that their limbs become numb and immobilized. If the skin gene is aware of its stem cell response, it can work with it.

As I mentioned, many athletes have skin genes as one of the dominant ones. Remember, we no longer have any pure 100% genes. Today we have a combination that would significantly impact the whole outlook; however, if we determined that the skin gene possesses a fair share in the combination.

All the described above take place. So if the skin gene is aware that they fight when stressed out, they fight not for the process of fighting. They fight to win, and psychological attention is released when they win.

Let's go back to the affective blocks. Winning is a phase of receiving, and once they win, they can relax for a little bit until tension rises again. If this method of relaxation becomes a go-to in the neural path of the person with the dominant skin gene, not only will it become an automatic reaction, but it also doesn't matter who the fight is with or for. It can be a college, a spouse or even a stranger on the bus.

Once it becomes a go-to relaxation tool, the person can attract or look for circumstances that involve a fight, sometimes even provoke a war with a person, even though they might have nothing to do with the source of tension stress for the skin gene. This is just one of the examples of how the shadow side of the skin gene might express itself during stressful situations.

After the Podium

Skin genes are also prone to taking action immediately, not their essence. Often this will cause silly mistakes and misunderstandings.

Waiting for the skin gene is torture. This is why the action isn't something other than an action to respond to. The activity can be moved. One of the most reactive things the skin gene can do. Some skim gene-dominant people under stress start pacing around the room, unconsciously imitating running.

Body movement is excellent for all genes, especially skin ones. It is their essence. Hence athletes are the essence of the skin gene. Another relaxing component is massage; since people with skin genes are susceptible to the skin's touch, they will love massage and caressing washing their skin, whether it's a bath, shower, or open water.

Such relaxing procedures have to become a routine in the skin genes' life so detention stays moderate rather than overwhelming when the stem cell will come to the rescue.

Also, keep in mind that the skin gene is about speed. They have explosive energy and do things fast and effectively, but they must rest in between. On the last, they have a powerful anal gene that accompanies the skin gene; these people are very prone to burnout if kept in work mode for too long.

For example, a skin gene can accomplish a month's work and sales in one week. That doesn't mean that if their anal boss steadily exploits them for four weeks straight, he'd get four months' worth of sales in one month and four years in one year.

I always use the same example when explaining this to students. Let's say we run 10K. The skin gene will run 400 meters Sprint, then rest, maybe walk, then dash 400 meters again and so on, until they cross the finish line of 10K. If an anal boss tells them to run 10K nonstop at the speed they're running 400 meters, they will die and most likely won't finish. So, both lose. The boss doesn't get the result, and the skin gene won't accomplish the desired outcome either. You can only imagine how poor former athletes with the dominant skin gene suffer in the modern work environment of 9-6, not knowing how they function. With two weeks of vacation a year, they dig an early grave for themselves.

They usually last about 5, maximum of seven years of such a work environment before a total collapse. And by collapsing, I mean broken families, mental and physical health, and a whole list of unpleasantries. They often think that for good enough pay, they can break their nature and make their bodywork for a few years, suffer through, before they release themselves from the prison of work with a good amount of cash in the bank.

These are usually former athletes who are so used to sacrificing in the name of big goals. Money for the skin gene is typically the number one priority. They want to make a certain amount before they marry, their children are born, and they retire.

When they're 35-37, they usually start pushing even more. Remember? The more stressed out the skin gene, the more effort they put into getting faster results so that they can release and relax. By that age, there are already quite exhausted from ongoing work and constant pressure and tension. T

hey plan to push a little more until they are, let's say, 45 years old, so they can finally retire with money in the bank because they can't go anymore.

During that time, they also become incredibly greedy, not only toward others but also toward themselves. They save money on vacations, even though they can afford a five-star hotel. They go to a three-star camp. Not because they like to camp but because it's cheaper. They give cheap gifts and look for free stuff to the point where they would go to friends' houses for visits, to have a free dinner, and to save money on food. The agenda is acquiring things without having to spend money on them or spend very little, as little as possible. Knowing they got it at the lowest price warms their souls and makes them relax and sleep at night. On the flip side, if they find out that someone got it even a dollar less, it will make them feel like they missed out and lost their sleep.

It wouldn't be so sad if they restricted themselves to the state. Still, most likely, their family, if by that time they didn't get fed up yet, will end up in a toxic environment of constant restriction, budgeting, saving for efficiency, and will suffer the pressure of counting every penny.

Unfortunately, people who encounter a stressed-out skin gene don't understand that they are in pain and need help. They think that the skin gene people are greedy Scrooge McDuck. So, they start distancing themselves from the skin gene, both friends and family, until the skin gene is left all alone.

Surprisingly even if the skin gene is at its lowest, they rarely feel lonely as long as they have money. They feel safer the more money they possess, especially today when money has so much power and control. You can buy almost anything. That way, the skin gene feels its power because it can make other people do what they want if they offer them the right amount.

The skin gene forgot its purpose in the tribe.

Historically the skin gene would conspire against the urethral gene to take the reins. And even if they succeeded, people would not accept them as rulers for too long and would throw a revolution.

Skin genes the lawmaker, which has always helped them to become lawyers. They love the law and the rules. Yet when the skin gene is stressed and not self-sufficient, we love to find loopholes in the law or blatantly cheat. Whether it's a sports game or a financial game.

Financial manipulations are one of the favourite stressed skin genes playgrounds. They are also the ones who gained the most satisfaction winning the case on the legalities. It's not fair, and they know it, but it doesn't matter to them as long as they are considered a winner.

Skin gene, when not fulfilled, is very possessive. They don't have "ours"; they have "mine." The Spirit of possessions gives them a sense of security and self-worth. Their smell can be repelled when the skin gene is distressed. So, to continue their gene lineage, they had to attract women and men with possessions. For example, anal genes, both men and women smell sturdy and reliable pheromones.

So, it is easier for them to attract a partner than for the skin gene. Naturally, the skin gene is not the most attractive pheromone-wise, so they practiced acquiring and even deceiving skills early. And we can't blame them for that. This is the way the gene learned to survive; it is what needed to be done for survival, no morals attached.

The gene can be "broken," and a person, especially children, might even become sick because they are not allowed to be who they are on the other side. If a parent noticed that the child stole or wanted something, it would offer the child a list of acceptable ways of acquiring things they want.

This way, the gene is preserved and can develop. When this child grows up, sure, acquiring items might become their motivation, but it will be done ingeniously and artfully. They would be the inventors of new businesses, new services etc. They would create workplaces and would allow other genes to shine, doing what they do best. This way, they work to better the tribe.

A broken gene might still build businesses. But these businesses will have a toxic culture, tax evasion and even financial scams.

I'm saying here that our genes don't go anywhere if we don't accept them. Every gene, in its developed condition, is a critical component of the tribe of our society. We need every gene. And every gene has its shadow side. There is no better or worse gene either. In its fulfilled condition, every one of them will make their host very happy. And every gene unattended and unfulfilled will pull the blanket requiring attention and attendance.

The acoustic gene would show signs of depression. Urethral will have kidney or bladder problems as well as genital viruses. Muscle genes will have muscle atrophy or muscle cramps. Visual will have anxiety and vision problems. The smell gene can become extremely antisocial and maniacal but might get a runny or stuffed nose. The list goes on.

After the Podium

Taking care of our nature is extremely important. In this case, the debate of nature versus nurture doesn't stand a chance. Because only if nature is nurtured do we have a mentally and physically healthy society. Today, however, people are programmed to hustle during the skin gene era. Suppose an anal gene tries to hustle and start a side business. In that case, it will fail because its perfectionism and analysis paralysis won't allow them to release even one product unless it reaches perfection. And that would take them years if not decades, and their product might become obsolete by then. They will only know how to sell it if they have a good portion of the skin gene or hire someone with a well-developed skin gene. Collaboration is key.

We are social animals for a reason. Social means interaction, teamwork, accommodation of differences and seeing the whole versus separate parts put together. Wouldn't you agree that car parts put together into a car is much more efficient than a pile of the same parts unattached to each other?

Recent statistics show that more than 20% of businesses fail in the first year, and nearly 50% fail in the first five years.

The numbers are even higher than that.

They are higher because people do what is not natural for them. They go to sales and business training, trying to train something they don't possess instead of cultivating what they have.

Valeria Tsoy

As athletes, we develop our strong sides. For example, an Alpine skier, a brilliant downhill racer with a urethral gene, won't spend months training for a slalom race if it's not their strongest skill and vice versa. When we look at it this way, it is obvious. Still, when we look at thousands of people wanting to become entrepreneurs, a profession marketed very vigorously over the past few decades, people don't question if that's who they are.

To their defence, I'll admit that the marketing machine (skin gene) is doing a great job selling to people, even if they don't need it. Marketing is there to convince buyers to buy what they don't need. Because if they truly needed it wouldn't require convincing.

Here we remember again the father of propaganda and his manipulative psychological techniques that gave life to mass marketing—starting with marketing cigarettes to women. Hence, they feel they possess the same social status as men. Skin gene has a different fairness. Just like anal and urethral have their own. Skin gene's fairness is "what I earned is mine" versus anal, "everyone gets an equal amount," and urethral, "everyone gets exactly as much as they need."

Of course, no wonder we see disagreements on the fairness of different societal actions. And everyone thinks their "fair" is better than other people's "fair."

After the Podium

Everyone who heard me speak about genes has asked me if I could develop a test where people can quickly determine their genes and save themselves time getting to know who they are and what they are made for.

And yet again, I will say that before we find out who we are and what genes have a stronger predisposition in our cells, we need to peel off all the expectations of right and wrong, perceptions, illusions, projections, and everything we know to get to the core, the essence of the genes. Genes have by far the most superior intellect than any brain ever will.

People are funny, and athletes are even funnier; they think they can control their bodies. They believe they can fight gravity, air resistance, natural cycles and even the need for the body to rest. Almost anything can improve, change, and extend with modern pharmaceutical, medical, and technological developments.

Yet when it comes to origins, our most significant strength is in giving in, when the lion eats meat and gives up veganism, when the bunny eats plants and gives up the carnivore diet.

Those advance who don't shy away from their nature and nurture their natural gift.

About the Author.

Drawing from a diverse range of disciplines, such as spirituality, psychology, neurobiology, and sociology, Valeria's work breaks down barriers and brings forth innovative solutions to this much-needed area of support.

Valeria Tsoy is an accomplished Olympic Snowboarder whose dedication to professional sports runs deep. With a passion for helping fellow athletes navigate the often-difficult transition after their competitive careers, she has devoted the past decade to researching the emotional and psychological impact of this phase.

Born into a family of athletes, Valeria has been involved in professional sports from a very young age, affording her a unique perspective and insight into the needs of her peers. Her work brings to light the lack of supportive structures available for modern athletes as they seek to mature mentally and emotionally as both individuals and members of society.

Val: val@valeriatsoy.com
778-994-84-75